COMFORT FOOD

COMFORT FOOD
Food to Make You Feel Good

MAUREEN SIMPSON

ABC BOOKS

For Ian, David and John

Published by ABC Books for the
AUSTRALIAN BROADCASTING CORPORATION
GPO Box 9994 Sydney NSW 2001

Copyright © Maureen Simpson 1998

First published 1998

All rights reserved. No part of this publication
may be reproduced, stored in a retrieval system
or transmitted in any form or by any means,
electronic, mechanical, photocopying, recording
or otherwise, without the prior written permission
of the Australian Broadcasting Corporation.

National Library of Australia
Cataloguing-in-Publication entry

Simpson, Maureen, 1933-,
 Comfort food: food to make you feel good: over 100
 flavour filled and easy-to-prepare recipes.
 Includes index.
 ISBN 0 7333 0618 7.
 1. Cookery. 2. Cookery, Australian. I. Australian
 Broadcasting Corporation. II. Title.
641.56

Designed by Eckermann Art and Design
Photography by Andrew Payne
Set in 12/14pt Leawood by Eckermann Art and Design
Colour separations by Hi Tech, Melbourne
Printed and bound in Australia by
Australian Print Group, Maryborough, Victoria

5 4 3 2 1

Contents

Acknowledgments	6
Author's Note	7
Temperature and conversion chart	8
Soups	9
Fish and Seafood	23
Mains	37
Vegetables and Salads	71
Snacks	99
Puddings	115
Biscuits, Cakes and Slices	137
Sauces and Stocks	153
Index	159

Acknowledgments

My special thanks

- To photographer, Andrew Payne who always takes such great photographs that capture the reality and texture of the food. Thank you for your clever lighting and for keeping your cool even though the temperature of the kitchen is soaring.
- To Margaret Ientile, for your inspirational ideas over the years we have worked together. Thank you for your expertise in assisting with the cooking for photography.
- To the many friends who generously gave me their treasured recipes, many of which are included in this book.

Author's Note

Comfort food is 'real food'. It is the kind of food we yearn for when away from home, or when life seems complicated and we need to eat something familiar with predictable flavours such as the special things our mothers cooked for us when we were feeling miserable or sick.

No matter how sophisticated the palate, it seems that everyone has at least one favourite dish from their childhood that evokes warm and comfortable feelings. Ask a group of people what 'comfort food' means to them and be prepared for a lively and enthusiastic reaction. I have posed this question many times while writing this book and it is always the same. There is a pause, followed by a far-away look, and then everyone starts talking at once, nominating anything from crumbed lamb cutlets or peanut butter sandwiches to soft-boiled eggs and toast soldiers. Predictably the initial response for some, especially during winter, is for soups, stews, home made pies and nursery puddings, complete with mouth-watering descriptions. And there seems to be a general consensus that 'you can't beat a good baked dinner'. For others, comfort food means rice, pasta, noodles, polenta ... and of course, potatoes, cooked almost every way you can imagine.

During summer, comfort food has a different meaning. With the abundance of fresh produce available, the desire to feast on succulent mangoes or simply a big bowl of salad is overwhelming, don't you agree? Sometimes it's a craving for the hot, spicy and exciting flavours in Laksa, Thai curries and stir-fried noodles, while at other times it just has to be good old-fashioned Salmon Patties all crusty and fragrant and straight from the pan. Easy to prepare meals enjoyed with friends, especially outdoors is another aspect of comfort food. The best entertaining is comfortable and non-threatening, using good produce (of which we have an abundance), treated simply so the fresh flavours dominate.

Cake is great comfort food. Have you ever noticed the hush that falls over a group of people when a really good chocolate cake is served? Conversation seems to stop in mid-sentence as the first portion is savoured (usually with eyes closed), followed immediately with beaming smiles and much nodding of heads.

Enjoy this book of recipes for the best comfort foods I know.

Handy Measuring Chart

Australian Metric Cup (250 mL)	Grams	Ounces (approx)	Australian Metric Cup (250 mL)	Grams	Ounces (approx)
butter	250 g	8¾ oz	chopped nuts, ground almonds	120 g	4¼ oz
flour – white *(lightly spooned into cup)*	135 g	4¾ oz	rice	220 g	7¾ oz
flour – wholemeal	145 g	5 oz	chopped chocolate	180 g	6¼ oz
flour – rye	115 g	4 oz	sugar – crystal	230 g	8 oz
cornflour	135 g	4¾ oz	sugar – caster	220 g	7¾ oz
rice flour	170 g	6 oz	brown sugar *(very firm pack)*	220 g	7¾ oz
cocoa	100 g	3½ oz	brown sugar *(light pack)*	150 g	5¼ oz
poppy seeds	150 g	5¼ oz	icing sugar *(well shaken down)*	150 g	5¼ oz
cornflakes	40 g	1⅓ oz	sweet biscuit crumbs	110 g	3¾ oz
rice bubbles	30 g	1 oz	breadcrumbs – fresh	60 g	2 oz
desiccated coconut, rolled oats	85 g	3 oz	breadcrumbs – fine dry	100 g	3½ oz
dried lentils, split peas, beans, chick peas	200 g	7 oz	breadcrumbs – Japanese-style	75 g	2½ oz
dried fruit – raisins, currants, sultanas	160 g	5¾ oz	cheese – hard *(parmesan, romano)*		
dates, apricots, dried, chopped	150 g	5¼ oz	freshly grated	90 g	3 oz
golden syrup, honey	360 g	12¾ oz	polenta	170 g	6 oz
jam *(approx, depending on type)*	320 g	11¼ oz	couscous	185 g	6½ oz

Tablespoons (20mL) Level Measures	Grams	Ounces (approx)	Tablespoons (20mL) Level Measures	Grams	Ounces (approx)
butter, peanut butter	20 g	⅔ oz	flour, cornflour	12 g	⅜ oz
baking powder	12 g	⅜ oz	dried yeast, nuts	10 g	⅓ oz
bi-carb soda	20 g	⅔ oz	golden syrup, honey	30 g	1 oz
gelatine	15 g	½ oz	salt, sugar – crystal	20 g	⅔ oz
rice *(approx)*	15 g	½ oz	sugar – caster, brown (firm pack)	15 g	½ oz
cocoa	7 g	¼ oz	yeast, fresh compressed	20 g	⅔ oz

Australian Standard Measures	
1 cup	250 mL
1 tablespoon	20 mL
1 teaspoon	5 mL

Oven Temperatures	Celsius	Fahrenheit
Very hot	230–250	450–500
Hot	200–210	400–425
Moderate to moderately hot	180–190	350–375
Slow to moderately slow	150–160	300–325
Very slow	120	250

If using a fan-forced oven the temperature may vary somewhere between 10–15°C less than the above temperatures. For the correct temperatures please check with your oven handbook.

Soups

Potato and Leek Soup

Pumpkin Soup

Pea and Ham Soup

French Onion Soup

Chicken and Vegetable Soup

Lamb Shank and Barley Broth

Beef Tea

Hirira

Quick and Easy Laksa Lemak

Tom Yum Goon

Won Ton Soup

POTATO AND LEEK SOUP

Serves 6

1 bunch leeks (about 3 leeks)
50 g butter
500 g potatoes (3 medium)
2 sticks celery, chopped
6 cups (1.5 litres) chicken stock
salt and freshly ground black pepper, to taste
chopped fresh chives and mint, to garnish
thick cream (optional)

Trim the leeks and wash thoroughly under cold, running water, then slice. Put into a large saucepan with the butter and cook over a very low heat for 5–10 minutes, stirring occasionally (the slow cooking develops a good flavour, but do take care to keep the heat very low so the leeks don't burn).

Peel the potatoes and cut into big cubes, then add to the soup with the celery. Add the chicken stock, then loosely cover the pot and allow the soup to simmer for about 30 minutes. Check the flavour, adding salt and pepper to taste.

To serve, ladle the soup into large, shallow soup plates and smother with chives and a little mint. Add a small dollop of cream to the centre of each serve if you wish.

BUTTERNUT PUMPKIN AND LEEK SOUP

Substitute 1 kg butternut pumpkin (peeled and chopped) for the potatoes and omit the celery. Cook the leeks in the butter first, then add the pumpkin and chicken stock. Simmer for about ¾ hour before blending to a puree with a food processor. Season with salt and pepper to taste, then thin the soup with a little milk if necessary. Heat thoroughly before ladling into large, shallow soup plates. Sprinkle a generous amount of chopped fresh chives over each serve.

Pumpkin Soup

Serves 6–8

1 kg pumpkin
30 g butter
1 onion, peeled and sliced
½ level teaspoon ground cumin
6 cups (1.5 litres) chicken stock or water
pinch of salt
salt and freshly ground black pepper, to taste
thick cream, for serving (optional)
chopped fresh chives, parsley or coriander

Peel the pumpkin and discard its seeds. Cut the pumpkin flesh into big chunks and set aside.

Melt the butter in a large, heavy saucepan. Add the onion and cook over a very low heat until it is soft and glossy; allow 5–10 minutes to develop a good flavour and take care not to burn (add a sprinkle of water to the onion if it is cooking too fast). Add the cumin and cook a minute longer, then add the chopped pumpkin, chicken stock and salt.

Bring to the boil then reduce the heat and cover the pot. Allow to simmer for 45 minutes or until the pumpkin is very tender. Smooth out the soup with a food processor (the hand-held food processor wands are excellent for this job).

Reheat the soup, add salt and pepper to taste and then serve the soup hot in individual serving bowls. Add a small spoonful of cream to each serve (if using), then sprinkle the chives, parsley or coriander over the top.

Pea and Ham Soup

Serves 8

2 cups (400 g) yellow split peas
1 onion, peeled and chopped (or grated)
2 large carrots, peeled and coarsely grated
2 sticks celery, chopped
1 ham hock or a meaty ham bone
10 cups (2.5 litres) water
2 pinches of dried thyme
salt and freshly ground black pepper, to taste
chopped fresh parsley and mint, to garnish

Put the split peas into a large saucepan or boiler. Add the onion, carrot, celery and ham hock. Pour in the water and add the thyme. The ham hock will supply some salt, so do not add any extra salt at this stage. Cover with a lid and bring to the boil. Simmer gently for about 2 hours. Stir occasionally during the last 30 minutes of cooking to make sure the soup doesn't catch on the bottom of the pot. Remove the ham hock, chop the meat and return to the soup, discarding any skin and bones. Skim away any fat from the surface of the soup, then season with a little salt and black pepper to taste. Serve hot, sprinkled with the fresh parsley and mint.

FRENCH ONION SOUP

Serves 6

6 medium brown onions, peeled and sliced
30 g butter
1½ tablespoons olive oil
1 heaped teaspoon brown sugar
2 level tablespoons plain flour
6 cups (1.5 litres) Rich Beef Stock (see page 157)
½ cup (125 mL) white wine
6 slices French bread
salt and freshly ground black pepper, to taste
1 cup grated Gruyère or Emmental cheese

Put the onion, butter and olive oil into a heavy-based saucepan. Cook over a very low heat, stirring often, for 30 minutes, until the onion is soft and glossy, and a rich, golden brown. This initial slow browning of the onion develops a good flavour and is essential for the success of the soup. Use a heat diffuser under the saucepan, if necessary, to keep the heat low, or add a tablespoon of water to the onion to stop it burning. When the onion is done, add the brown sugar and cook for a minute or so more. Sprinkle in the flour, stir well, then stir in the Rich Beef Stock and white wine. Continue stirring until the soup reaches the boil, then reduce the heat and simmer gently for 30 minutes.

Meanwhile, preheat the oven to 180°C (350°F). Place the slices of bread on a baking tray and bake in the oven for 20 minutes, or until crisp and golden. Do not turn the oven off. Taste the onion soup, then season to taste with salt and pepper. Pour into a casserole dish or 6 individual soup ramekins. Float the bread on top of the soup, then sprinkle over the cheese and bake in the oven for a further 10 minutes. Serve the soup immediately.

Chicken and Vegetable Soup

Serves 6

Make your own chicken stock for 'real' chicken flavour.

1 bunch spring onions (white part only), finely chopped
2 sticks celery, finely chopped
1 level tablespoon butter
8 cups (2 litres) homemade Chicken Stock (see following)
2 carrots, finely diced
3 medium potatoes, finely diced
1 chicken breast fillet or 2 thigh fillets, diced
40 g fine pasta (tagliolini, vermicelli etc) or use 2 level tablespoons rice
500 g diced mixed vegetables (see suggestions following)
1 ripe tomato, chopped
2 tablespoons chopped fresh parsley, plus extra for serving
salt and freshly ground black pepper, to taste
chopped fresh chives, for serving

Put the spring onions and the celery into a large saucepan with the butter. Cook over a low heat, stirring occasionally, for a few minutes. Add the chicken stock and bring to the boil.

Add the carrot and potato to the pot with the chicken. Break the pasta into small pieces (this is important, otherwise the soup is too hard to eat) and add to the soup. Return the soup to the boil, then simmer for 10 minutes.

Add the mixed vegetables, tomato and parsley. Season to taste with a little salt and cook for a further 5 minutes, or until the pasta is tender and the vegetables are cooked sufficiently. Serve in large, shallow soup dishes, sprinkled with the extra parsley and chives. Season each serve with a generous quantity of freshly ground black pepper.

Note: Suitable vegetables to add during the last five minutes of cooking are finely sliced green beans, snow peas, button mushrooms or spinach; diced zucchini or pumpkin and young fresh or frozen green peas.

CHICKEN STOCK

Makes 3 litres

4 chicken frames or 2 kg chicken necks (buy at poultry shop)
2 chicken Marylands (drumstick and thigh)
1 onion, peeled and halved
1 stick celery, halved
½ cup (125 mL) white wine (optional)
16 cups (4 litres) water
1 teaspoon peppercorns
½ bay leaf
few sprigs of fresh parsley
½ teaspoon dried thyme
thin strip of lemon rind

Place all the ingredients in a boiler or large saucepan (do not add any salt). Cover loosely with a lid and simmer for 1½–2 hours. Strain and refrigerate immediately. Skim off any fat from the surface of the stock. Use as required. Any leftover stock should be stored in a labelled airtight container in the freezer. Stir the leftover stock before freezing.

Lamb Shank and Barley Broth

Serves 6

3 lamb shanks (ask butcher to saw shanks into halves)
10 cups (2.5 litres) water
¼ cup pearl barley
1 large onion, peeled and chopped
2 large carrots, peeled and diced
1 parsnip, peeled and diced
2 sticks celery, sliced
1 large ripe tomato, finely chopped
½ level teaspoon salt
½ cup chopped fresh parsley
freshly ground black pepper, to taste

Put the lamb shanks, water, pearl barley, onion, carrots, parsnip, celery and tomato into a large saucepan or boiler. Bring to the boil, then skim off any scum from the surface and side of the pot. Add the salt and half the parsley, then cover the pot loosely with a lid and simmer for 1½ hours, adding extra water if necessary. Remove the lamb shanks, chop the meat and return to the broth, discarding the bones. Skim away any fat from the surface of the broth. Serve the piping hot soup in large, shallow soup plates. Season to taste with black pepper and sprinkle with the remaining chopped parsley. Store any leftovers in the refrigerator.

Note: You can make this soup a few hours ahead of time. Refrigerate as soon as possible after cooking, then skim away all fat from the top before reheating.

Beef Tea

Serves 4

A nourishing soup with gentle flavours to make for someone you love who's in need of some nurturing. My mother always made this for me whenever I was sick and now I make it for my family.

750 g to 1 kg gravy beef (shin of beef), preferably in one piece
1 level tablespoon plain flour
2 level tablespoons pearl barley
1 small white onion, peeled and very finely chopped
10 cups (2.5 litres) water
1 level teaspoon salt
extra salt and freshly ground black pepper, to taste
finely chopped fresh parsley, for serving

Trim and discard any fat from the beef, then cut the meat into two or three chunks. Roll in flour (this prevents the broth from separating). Put into a large saucepan with the pearl barley, onion, water and salt. Bring to the boil, then reduce the heat to as low as possible and cover the pot with a lid. The secret of success for a rich beef flavour is to pierce the meat from time to time with two forks to release the juices. Cook for 2–3 hours, adding extra water if the liquid evaporates too much. Remove the beef from the soup, chop the choicest pieces finely and return to the saucepan. Season with a little black pepper and a little extra salt if you think it needs it. Serve the beef and barley broth with a small quantity of meat in each bowl, then sprinkle each serve with the parsley. Accompany with thin slices of good white bread.

Note: The leftover meat could be chopped finely and used to make a small bowl of brawn (see page 102).

Hirira

Serves 10

This spicy Moroccan soup makes a warm and nourishing winter meal. Add lemon juice and mint at serving time for a fresh, lively flavour.

750 g lamb shoulder meat or lean stewing chops
½ level teaspoon ground turmeric
2 level teaspoons ground coriander
1–2 level teaspoons ground black pepper
3 level teaspoons ground cumin
2 medium brown onions, peeled and chopped
2 tablespoons olive oil
2 sticks celery, sliced
500 g fresh ripe tomatoes, chopped
50 g sachet tomato paste (optional)
2 cups brown lentils
12 cups (3 litres) water
1 bay leaf
1 stick cinnamon
½ cup fresh coriander leaves
½ cup fresh parsley leaves
1½ level teaspoons salt
good pinch of saffron threads, soaked in 1 tablespoon warm water
2 x 425 g cans chickpeas, drained
2–3 lemons, cut into wedges
fresh mint leaves, for serving

Trim and discard any fat from the lamb. Chop the meat into small cubes then put into a suitable container for marinating. Sprinkle with the turmeric, coriander, pepper and cumin, and mix well. Cover and refrigerate for 30 minutes (or overnight).

To make the soup, put the onion into a large saucepan or boiler with the olive oil. Cook over a low heat for 5 minutes or so, until the onion is soft and glossy. Add the marinated lamb and brown lightly, releasing the tantalising aroma of the spices. Now add the celery, tomatoes, tomato paste (if using) and lentils.

Pour in the water, then add the bay leaf and cinnamon.

Bring to the boil then add the coriander, parsley, salt and soaked saffron. Cover the saucepan with a lid and simmer for about one hour. Add the chickpeas and cook for a further 15 minutes.

Serve hot in large bowls with juicy lemon wedges and fresh mint leaves. The juice from the lemon wedges is squeezed over the soup. Serve with warm crusty rolls or Turkish bread.

Using dried chickpeas: Soak 1 cup dried chickpeas in a bowl of cold water overnight. Drain the chickpeas and put into a saucepan. Cover well with fresh water and cook until tender, about 2 hours (or 20 minutes in a pressure cooker). Add to the soup and simmer for an extra 15 minutes.

Quick and Easy Laksa Lemak

Serves 4

½ x 260 g bottle Reuben Solomon's Singapore Laksa Paste
4 cups (1 litre) chicken stock (if using packet stock, use 2 cups *each* stock and water)
100 g dried rice vermicelli noodles
600 g uncooked medium king prawns, peeled and deveined
300–400 mL can coconut milk or coconut cream
laksa garnishes (see following)

Put the laksa paste into a large saucepan with the chicken stock and bring to the boil. Add the dried rice vermicelli and boil for 3 minutes. Now add the prawns and cook for a few minutes, just until the prawns change colour, then stir in the coconut milk and heat through. If the laksa is too hot for your taste, add more coconut milk. Serve in large Chinese soup bowls with a selection of garnishes. Choose from the following:

- Chopped cucumber, finely sliced young spring onions (green part only), fresh mint, fresh coriander, Vietnamese mint (also known as laksa leaf) and lightly blanched bean sprouts. (Put the trimmed bean sprouts into a colander then pour over boiling water.)
- Quail eggs. Boil for 3–5 minutes then cool quickly under cold, running water. Peel carefully (they're sometimes hard to peel). Substitute hard-boiled hen eggs, quartered, if you do not like quail eggs or find it difficult to buy them.
- Fried tofu. Cut tofu into large squares — use long-life tofu or fresh firm tofu. Dust with flour, deep-fry in oil until golden then drain and slice. Tofu is best when prepared just before serving.
- Chilli oil. Pour a little chilli oil on top of each serve.
- Fried onions. Peel and thinly slice Spanish onions, then fry slowly in vegetable oil until a rich, golden brown. Allow to drain on paper towels before serving.

Note: The laksa paste used in this recipe is made in Australia and available at large department stores and delicatessens.

Tom Yum Goon

Thai Hot and Sour Prawn Soup

Serves 6

6 cups (1.5 litres) chicken or prawn stock (see page 158)
1 bunch of coriander
2 stalks lemon grass (white bulb-end only)
3 or 4 slices fresh or dried galangal
3 kaffir lime leaves (fresh or dried)
6 black or white peppercorns, crushed
2 chillies, seeded and thinly sliced
750 g raw prawns, peeled and deveined (reserve prawn heads for stock, see following)
125 g small, firm button mushrooms, sliced
6 spring onions (white part only), thinly sliced (reserve some green stems for garnish)
2 tablespoons fish sauce nam pla
2 tablespoons fresh lime juice

Put the stock into a saucepan. Remove the roots from the coriander, scrub well, then chop finely and add to the stock (reserve the coriander leaves). Smash the ends of the lemon grass with a meat mallet or large kitchen knife and add to the saucepan along with sliced galangal, 2 kaffir lime leaves and the peppercorns. Bring to the boil, then reduce the heat and simmer for 20 minutes.

Strain the broth and return it to the saucepan. Add the chillies, prawns, mushrooms and spring onion. Chop most of the reserved coriander leaves and add to the broth. Simmer for about 2 minutes, until the prawns are cooked. Add the fish sauce and lime juice, and stir well. Serve immediately in big, deep bowls, garnished with the remaining coriander leaves, finely sliced spring onion stems and remaining kaffir lime leaf, sliced into the finest possible shreds.

Note: If the broth separates after adding the lime juice, don't worry. Just give the soup a good stir, heat thoroughly and serve immediately.

Prawn Stock
Makes 6 cups (1.5 litres)

Rinse the prawn heads under cold, running water then put into a large saucepan with 2 teaspoons of light vegetable oil. Toss over a medium heat until pink. Pour in 7 cups (1.75 litres) of water and simmer for 20 minutes. Strain and measure. Make up to 1.5 litres with water if necessary.

Won Ton Soup

Serves 4–6

6 cups (1.5 litres) chicken stock
5 cm chunk green ginger, peeled and sliced
2 young spring onions, tied in a knot
1 clove garlic, peeled
1 tablespoon light soy sauce
Won Ton Dumplings (see below)
salt, to taste
sesame oil
extra young spring onion (green part only), finely sliced
fresh coriander leaves

Skim any fat from the top of the stock and discard. Bring the stock to the boil in a large, deep saucepan with the ginger, spring onion, garlic and soy sauce. Simmer for 20 minutes, then scoop out the ginger, garlic and spring onion.

Drop in the Won Ton Dumplings and simmer for 5–7 minutes, until they float to the top (check one to make sure it's cooked). Check the soup for salt, adding a little if necessary, then add 1 teaspoon of the sesame oil.

Put a generous quantity of the extra spring onion and some coriander leaves in the bottom of each large Chinese soup bowl. Ladle in the hot soup and serve sprinkled with more spring onion, coriander leaves, and a dash of sesame oil.

Won Ton Dumplings

350 g large raw king prawns, peeled and deveined (about 10)
250 g pork fillet
good pinch of salt
2 tablespoons finely chopped spring onions (white part only)
1 small egg
1 packet (40) Shanghai-style won ton wrappers

Mince prawns and pork in a food processor with the salt, then add spring onion and egg and process briefly, until thoroughly mixed. Alternatively, chop the prawns, pork and spring onion very finely, then combine with the egg. Put a small teaspoonful of the mixture on the centre of each won ton wrapper, then gather the wrapper around the filling. Pinch tightly to seal so each dumpling resembles a little money bag. Refrigerate until ready to use.

Note: Three or four canned water chestnuts, very finely chopped, could be added.

Fish and Seafood

Prawn and Fresh Herb Risotto

Seafood Paella

Scallop and Prawn Mornay

Salmon Patties

Greek Prawns with Feta

Char-grilled Swordfish

Fish and Chips

Fish Curry

Prawn and Fresh Herb Risotto

Serves 4

This is a basic recipe for a seafood risotto. Once you've mastered the art, you can vary the ingredients depending on what you have in the pantry.

600 g medium king prawns, peeled and deveined
(reserve heads for stock (optional) — see Note)
3½ (875 mL) cups prawn stock
2 cups (500 mL) fish stock
2 tablespoons olive oil
1 level tablespoon butter
1 onion, peeled and finely chopped
2 large cloves garlic, crushed
2 cups Arborio rice
½ cup (125 mL) white wine
good pinch of saffron threads
2 tablespoons chopped fresh parsley
2 tablespoons chopped fresh chives
salt and freshly ground black pepper, to taste

Rinse the reserved prawn heads under cold, running water, then put into a saucepan with a strip of lemon peel. Cover well with water and simmer for 20 minutes. Strain, then measure. Make up to 3½ cups with extra water if necessary. Add the fish stock (making a total of 5½ cups boiling stock). Make sure the stock is boiling in a pot on the cooktop, so that it is close at hand to the saucepan with the rice.

Put the oil and butter into a large, heavy-based saucepan with the onion and garlic. Cook over a low heat, stirring occasionally, until the onion is soft. Add the rice and stir with a wooden spoon. Now add the wine and saffron, stirring constantly. Over a medium heat, add a couple of ladles of the boiling stock to the rice, and stir with a wooden spoon to mix it through well. The stock should be absorbed into the rice before adding more. Add the boiling stock as necessary, one ladle at a time, and give the pan a little stir occasionally to make sure the rice doesn't stick to the bottom. The cooking time is about 20 minutes; be careful not to overcook.

Saute the peeled prawns (chop if large) in an extra tablespoon of butter or oil, then add the parsley and chives. Stir through the risotto, then season to taste with salt and black pepper.

Note: If making prawn head stock is not your idea of a good time, use 2 × 500 mL bought stock and add 1½ cups water to make up to 5½ cups.

Hint: Make sure you use a medium heat under the saucepan. If the heat is too high, the liquid will evaporate too quickly, leaving the rice undercooked. If too low, the rice could become gluggy.

Seafood Paella

Serves 8

2 large, ripe tomatoes
100 mL olive oil
4 cloves garlic, peeled and finely sliced or crushed
1 large onion, peeled and sliced
1 kg raw prawns, peeled and deveined
500 g calamari hoods, sliced into rings
600 g thick fish fillets, skinned and cut into chunks
400 g Calasparra or Arborio rice
$3^1/_2$ cups (875 mL) fish stock
$^1/_2$ teaspoon saffron threads dissolved in 1 tablespoon warm water
1 level teaspoon salt
1 kg black mussels, scrubbed
$^1/_2$ cup (125 mL) white wine
freshly ground black pepper, to taste
$^1/_2$ cup chopped parsley

Grate the tomatoes into a small saucepan, discarding the skin. Add 2 teaspoons of the olive oil, then simmer until the tomatoes are reduced to a thick red purée. Set aside.

To make the paella, heat half the remaining oil in a paella pan. Add the garlic and onion, and cook gently for a few minutes. Increase the heat slightly and add the prawns and calamari. Cook for a few minutes, then remove to a plate. Add the chunks of fish to the pan and fry until lightly cooked, about 5 minutes. Transfer the fish to the plate with the prawns, then cover with foil to keep hot.

Add the remaining oil to the paella pan, then add the rice. Stir over a medium heat to coat the grains with the oil. Add the reserved tomato purée, fish stock, saffron mixture and salt. Mix well, then reduce the heat and cook for about 18 minutes. Turn off the heat. Use a wooden paddle to loosen the rice underneath once or twice during cooking, but do not stir as this can break up the rice grains.

Meanwhile, put the mussels into a large saucepan with the wine. Bring to the boil and stir occasionally until the shells open, about 5 minutes. Arrange the mussels and remaining cooked seafood on the rice mixture, then drizzle with the strained mussel juices. Season generously with black pepper and sprinkle with the parsley. Cover paella with foil to keep hot prior to serving.

To prepare mussels scrub under cold, running water, discarding any mussels that remain open even after handling. To store prior to cooking, place the mussels in a large bowl in the refrigerator. Use within one day (two at the most).

Calasparra is a variety of large, short-grained rice imported from Spain. It becomes plump and juicy when cooked, and is perfect for paella. Arborio rice or short-grain Australian Calrose rice could be substituted.

Grated tomato is a quick way to add a fresh tomato purée directly to the dish you are cooking. This is how it's done. Cut ripe tomato into halves, then rub the cutside onto the coarse blades of a hand-held grater, gradually flattening your hand as you reach the skin.

The paella pan is traditionally a large, shallow pan, which allows the rice to cook quickly without becoming soggy.

Scallop and Prawn Mornay

Serves 6

This is my husband's favourite meal. Whenever he needs a little cheering up (or I want to get into the good books), I make this dish. The family love it, too, so it sometimes appears as an entrée for Christmas lunch.

750 g Tasmanian or Victorian scallops
¾ cup (190 mL) dry white wine
¾ cup (190 mL) water
1 teaspoon fennel seeds
½ teaspoon black peppercorns
1 small bunch spring onions (white part only), chopped
60 g butter
250 g small, firm button mushrooms, sliced
3 level tablespoons plain flour
2¼ cups (565 mL) milk
2 tablespoons crème fraîche or cream
1 level teaspoon tomato paste
½ teaspoon dried tarragon
tiny pinch of cayenne pepper
salt, to taste
750 g cooked prawns, peeled and deveined
1 tablespoon chopped fresh parsley
buttered crumbs (see following)
2 lemons, cut into wedges

Remove and discard the black thread from the scallops. Put the scallops into a saucepan with the wine, water, fennel seeds, peppercorns and 1 tablespoon of the spring onions. Bring slowly to a simmer, then turn off heat and leave for one minute (no longer or the scallops will shrink). Remove the scallops with a slotted spoon, then place into a dish and reserve. Boil the scallop liquid rapidly until reduced by half, to concentrate the marvellous flavour. Strain (you should have about ¾ cup). Set aside.

Melt the butter in a wide, shallow saucepan, add the remaining spring onions and the mushrooms. Cook quickly for a few minutes, stirring often, until the mushrooms soften. Add the flour and mix in well to make a roux. Add ¾ cup of reserved scallop liquid and 1½ cups of the milk. Bring to the boil, stirring constantly, then beat to make the sauce very smooth and shiny. Stir in the crème fraiche, tomato paste, tarragon, and a tiny pinch of cayenne (be careful, cayenne is very hot). Season with salt to taste then add the cooked scallops, prawns and parsley. Add enough of the remaining milk to thin down to make a light sauce. Divide this mixture between six buttered ovenproof scallop shells or shallow gratin dishes. Cover the top with buttered crumbs then refrigerate until ready to serve.

Preheat the oven to 220°–230°C (425°–450°F). Reheat the mornay until the sauce is bubbling and the crumbs are crisp and golden. Serve with wedges of lemon.

Buttered crumbs: Mix 1 heaped cup soft white breadcrumbs with 1 tablespoon melted butter and a few drops garlic juice (squeeze garlic clove in a crusher to release a few drops of juice for a subtle flavour).

Salmon Patties

Serves 4–6

Serve the salmon patties hot and crusty from the pan, with a dollop of Tartare Sauce or mayonnaise and chopped chives — yum!

---

600 g (4–5 medium-sized) potatoes
2 x 210 g cans red salmon (or 1 x 210 g can and 1 x 105 g can red salmon), drained
1 small white salad onion, peeled and finely chopped or grated (see Note)
4 spring onions (white part only), finely chopped
2 tablespoons chopped fresh parsley
¼ lemon
1 egg
salt and freshly ground black pepper, to taste
plain flour, for dusting
beaten egg (optional)
dry breadcrumbs (optional)
2–3 tablespoons light vegetable oil, for frying
1–2 lemons, cut into wedges
Tartare Sauce (see page 35) or mayonnaise and chives, for serving

Peel the potatoes, cut into chunks and put into a saucepan with sufficient water to cover the potatoes. Put the lid on the pan, bring to the boil and simmer for 20–25 minutes. Drain and mash the potato very well before putting in a mixing bowl. Add the salmon, salad onion, spring onion, parsley, a tiny squeeze of lemon juice and the egg. Mix well, then season with salt and pepper to taste. Give the mixture a good beat with a wooden spoon. Cover the bowl then chill the mixture in the refrigerator for at least 30 minutes before cooking.

To make the patties, take heaped tablespoons of the chilled mixture and roll into balls with floured hands. Pat down into flat cakes, about 2 cm thick. The mixture should make about 12 patties. Dust lightly with flour (if you like crumbed patties dip into beaten egg and then dry breadcrumbs).

Heat the light vegetable oil in a large, shallow frying pan over a medium heat. Add some of the patties, leaving room between for turning (don't crowd the pan — cook in batches or use two pans). Cook until golden, then turn over and cook the other side (see hints following). When cooked on both sides, drain the patties on paper towels. Serve hot with lemon wedges and topped with a spoonful of Tartare Sauce or mayonnaise and chives. Accompany with one green vegetable (beans are good) or with a salad.

Note: If you prefer, fry the onion in a little butter or oil to soften before adding to the mixture.

Hints

Many good cooks often complain that their salmon patties break up in the pan when they try to turn them over. Here are some tips for success.
- Make sure that you cook the potatoes sufficiently and mash them well so that they are free of lumps.
- Chill the patty mixture so that it firms up before cooking.
- Don't make the patties too thin — they should be at least 2 cm thick.
- Don't crowd the pan. Leave plenty of room between the patties so that they can be turned easily. A shallow pan is best for turning the patties.
- Don't be in too much of a hurry to turn them over, especially if making patties without the breadcrumb coating. Let them form a thin, crisp coating underneath before attempting to cook the other side.
- Crumbed patties are easier to cook because they're held together with the crusty coating, but take care not to have the oil too hot because they can burn easily.

TUNA AND FRESH CORIANDER PATTIES

Substitute canned tuna for the salmon and use fresh coriander leaves instead of the parsley. Add 2 tablespoons *very finely* chopped celery, 1 teaspoon grated fresh ginger and a dash of sweet chilli sauce.

Greek Prawns with Feta

Serves 4

A lovely dish to serve for an alfresco lunch on a balmy autumn day.

1 kg large raw king prawns, peeled and deveined
1 medium onion, peeled and finely chopped
2 large cloves garlic, peeled and crushed
4 tablespoons olive oil
4 large, ripe tomatoes (650 g), peeled and chopped (or use 1½ x 425 g cans whole tomatoes)
2 level teaspoons tomato paste
1 cup (250 mL) dry white wine
¼ cup chopped fresh parsley, plus extra for serving
1 level teaspoon dried oregano or Greek rigani
pinch of sugar
pinch of salt
125 g feta cheese, cut into small cubes
freshly cracked black pepper (optional)

Wash the prawns in cold water and pat dry.

Put the onion and garlic in a large frying pan with the olive oil. Cook gently for 5–10 minutes over a very low heat, stirring occasionally. Add the tomatoes, tomato paste, white wine, parsley and oregano. Add the sugar and salt, then simmer for about 20 minutes to create a tomato sauce (add a dash of water if the sauce evaporates too much).

Add the prawns, then cover the pan and cook for about 5 minutes, until the prawns are 'just' cooked. Add the feta and cook for a minute or so longer, just long enough for the feta to heat through.

Serve immediately, sprinkled with the extra parsley and some freshly cracked pepper if you wish. Accompany with warm, crusty bread rolls to mop up the juices. Finish with a big green salad.

Lamb Shank and Barley Broth (page 16)

Hirira (page 18)

Greek Prawns with Feta (page 32)

Char-grilled Swordfish (page 33) and Caponata (page 83)

Chicken Pie (page 50)

Stir-fried Chicken & Noodles (page 49)

Easy Lasagne (page 62)

Shepherd's Pie (page 59)

Char-grilled Swordfish

Serves 4–6

Sword fish has a delicious flavour and is very juicy if cooked briefly, so take care not to overcook it.

4–6 swordfish cutlets (1.5–2 cm thick)
3 tablespoons olive oil
1 tablespoon of fresh lemon juice
1 clove garlic, peeled and smashed with side of knife
6 sprigs of fresh marjoram
freshly ground black pepper and salt, to taste

Put the fish into a shallow dish and add the oil, lemon juice, garlic and marjoram. Turn the fish in this mixture to coat it, then cover and refrigerate for at least 30 minutes before cooking. Heat a ribbed grill-pan until smoking hot, then add the fish cutlets and cook for about 2 minutes on one side. Turn and cook the second side for about 1 minute, or until 'just' cooked and still juicy. The cooking time depends on the thickness of the cutlets, so adjust the time accordingly, but try not to overcook them. Sword fish is similar to tuna in that it is best when briefly cooked. Season with a generous quantity of black pepper and a little salt. Serve immediately with vegetables or salad.

Note: Caponata (see page 83) is a delicious Italian salad to serve with char-grilled fish.

Fish and Chips

Serves 6

Fresh fish in a light batter served straight from the pan while still crisp and crunchy is hard to beat, especially if teamed with home-made Tartare Sauce and really good chips.

1.5 kg fish fillets (such as flathead, bream, ocean perch or snapper)
1 cup self-raising flour
1 level tablespoon cornflour
good pinch of salt
1 tablespoon light oil
1 cup (250 mL) cold water
squeeze of lemon juice
light oil (extra), for frying
salt and freshly ground black pepper, to taste
little extra flour, for dusting
lemon wedges, to serve
Tartare Sauce (see page 35)
Potato Chips (see page 35)

Skin fish and remove any bones with tweezers. Put fish onto a plate, cover loosely and refrigerate until ready to cook.

To make the crisp batter, sift the flour, cornflour and salt into a mixing bowl. Make a well in the centre, then add the oil and ¾ cup of the water. Beat with a wooden spoon to smooth out any lumps, add a good squeeze of lemon juice and the remaining water. The batter should be a light consistency; add an extra tablespoon of water if it seems a little thick.

Heat sufficient light oil to deep-fry the fish in a wok, deep frying pan or automatic fryer.

Season the fish fillets with salt and pepper, dust with the extra flour then dip into the batter (let excess batter drain off for a few seconds). Lower the battered fish slowly into the hot oil. Fry until the batter is golden and the fish is cooked through, then drain on crumpled paper towels. Serve immediately with lemon wedges, Tartare Sauce and freshly made Potato Chips. Accompany with vegetables in season (green beans are nice) or a salad and fresh bread and butter.

Potato Chips

Serves 6

The best potatoes to use for chips are Russet Burbank (Idaho), Kennebec, Pontiac, Bintje, Spunta, Delaware and King Edward. Use fresh oil and double-fry, increasing the heat during the last frying to make them crisp and golden.

6 large potatoes
fresh oil, for deep frying
salt, for serving

Scrub potatoes (if cooking with skins on), or peel them. Cut into long, thick chips. Soak in a basin of cold, salted water until ready to cook. Heat sufficient oil to deep-fry the chips in a large saucepan, wok or automatic fryer. Meanwhile, dry the potatoes well in a clean towel. Fry the chips in two or three batches, using a medium heat to start so potatoes are almost cooked, then remove and drain well on crumpled paper towels. Reheat oil until smoking hot and return the chips briefly to the oil until crisp and golden brown. Remove from the oil immediately and drain briefly. Sprinkle with a little salt and serve straight away.

Tartare Sauce

Serves 6

2 spring onions
2 teaspoons capers
2 teaspoons finely chopped gherkin
1 tablespoon finely chopped parsley
½ cup mayonnaise
good squeeze of lemon juice
salt and freshly ground black pepper, to taste

Trim the spring onions, discarding most of the green stems. Chop the white part of the spring onions finely and put into a small mixing bowl with the capers, gherkin, parsley and mayonnaise. Mix well. Add a good squeeze of lemon juice and season with a little salt and pepper. Cover and refrigerate for 30 minutes before using so the flavours mingle.

Fish Curry

Serves 4

Fish fillets in a fragrant curry that's not too hot.

---

1 kg thick fish fillets (such as ocean perch, orange roughy, coral trout or ling)
2 tablespoons fresh lime juice
½ level teaspoon salt
1 level tablespoon mild curry powder
½ level teaspoon ground turmeric
1 level teaspoon dried chilli flakes
1 tablespoon melted butter or oil
1 small onion, peeled and finely chopped
1 level teaspoon grated fresh ginger
1 clove garlic, crushed
1 ripe tomato, peeled and finely chopped
1 stalk lemon grass (trim away green leaves)
1 medium-sized green or red chilli
1 x 270 mL can coconut milk
freshly ground black pepper, to taste
fresh coriander leaves, for serving
lime wedges, for serving

Skin the fish fillets and remove any bones with tweezers. Place in a large, flat dish in a single layer. Sprinkle the fish with the lime juice and salt, then sprinkle over the curry powder, turmeric and chilli flakes. Let stand for 5 minutes or so.

Meanwhile put butter in a large frying pan. Add the onion and cook over a low heat until the onion is soft and glossy, then add the ginger, garlic and tomato. Split the lemon grass stem in half and add to the pan with the chilli. Cook for a few minutes longer, then add the fish (and any juices from the dish). Pour in the coconut milk and cook the fish gently in this mixture for about 5 minutes, or until cooked through, turning only once. Discard lemon grass.

Season with a little black pepper and scatter over fresh coriander leaves. Serve with plain boiled rice and juicy lime wedges. Accompany with briefly cooked bright green snow peas, pappadams and slivered fresh mango or a fresh mango salsa.

Mains

Roast Fillet of Beef
Rich Beef Casserole
My Mother's Meat Pie
Italian Roast Chicken
Crumbed Chicken
Juicy Roast Tarragon Chicken
Thai Chicken Curry
Stir-fried Chicken & Noodles
Chicken Pie
Greek Roast Lamb with Lemon
Irish Stew
Lamb Curry
Baked Dinner
Lamb Chop and Potato bake
Shepherd's Pie
Savoury Mince
Spaghetti Bolognaise
Easy Lasagne
Margaret's Meat Balls in Tomato Sauce
Pork Sausages in Tomato and Cumin Gravy
Pork in Peanut Satay Sauce
Roast Pork with Crackling
Veal Casserole
Veal and Mushroom Stew
Pot Roast of Veal with Mushroom Sauce

Roast Fillet of Beef

Serves 6–7

2 whole butt-end fillets of beef, about 625 g each
1 tablespoon butter
1 tablespoon olive oil
freshly ground black pepper
Béarnaise Sauce, to serve (see below)

Preheat the oven to 200°C (400°F). Trim the beef, then, using a small, sharp knife, strip away the thin membrane covering the fillets. For a good shape, tie the fillets in a few places with white string.

Heat the butter and olive oil together in a large frying pan. When smoking hot, add the whole beef fillets and seal them quickly, turning with tongs. When the fillets are browned all over, transfer to a small baking dish, season generously with black pepper and bake in the hot oven for about 25 minutes. This timing is for medium-rare. Allow 5 minutes either way according to taste. Remove from the oven and let stand in a warm place near the stove for 5 minutes to allow the meat to 'rest'.

Meanwhile, add about ½ cup water to the meat juices in the baking dish. Stir on top of the stove until boiling, then season with salt. Cut the beef into thick slices to serve on hot plates and moisten with the gravy. Accompany with tiny new potatoes (the smallest you can find) and lashings of Béarnaise Sauce to melt deliciously over the meat and potatoes. Freshly cooked green beans would the perfect accompaniment with this dish.

Béarnaise Sauce

Serves 6

Traditionalists may scoff, but this recipe works beautifully in the microwave and is very easy to make. Béarnaise Sauce is delicious with roast beef, grilled steak, lamb chops, char-grilled scallops and new potatoes.

2 tablespoons water
2 tablespoons vinegar (white or brown, or a mixture of both)
3 spring onions (white part only), very finely chopped

good pinch of dried tarragon
125 g butter
3 egg yolks
salt and freshly ground black pepper, to taste
good pinch of very finely chopped fresh parsley

Easy Microwave Method: Put the water, vinegar, spring onions and tarragon into a small heatproof, microwave-safe bowl. Microwave on high for 3 minutes. Add the butter and microwave on high for 1 minute. Remove from the microwave, add the egg yolks and whisk well. Set the microwave to defrost and cook for a further 60–80 seconds, stopping the oven every 20 seconds to whisk the sauce. I usually find that it takes 70–80 seconds to thicken, but as all ovens vary, it is best to be careful since the sauce can curdle if overcooked. Remove from the oven and whisk well. Season with a tiny pinch of salt and pepper, then stir in a good pinch of very finely chopped parsley. Let the sauce stand for a few minutes before serving.

Traditional Method: Place the water, vinegar, spring onions and tarragon into a small saucepan and simmer over a very low heat until reduced in volume by half. Strain into a small heatproof basin. Add the egg yolks and whisk well. Place over a pan of gently simmering water and beat until the sauce starts to thicken. Melt the butter and add to the sauce *drop by drop*, beating all the time. Remove from the heat and stir in the parsley, salt and pepper.

Note: If you want to make the sauce an hour or two before dinner, then simply pour the finished sauce into a serving dish, cover with food wrap and keep at room temperature. The sauce can be served at room temperature (it melts over the meat anyway). If you want to reheat the sauce, microwave on defrost for about 10 seconds.

RICH BEEF CASSEROLE

Serves 6–8

The beef is incredibly tender when cooked slowly in its rich red wine sauce.

---

150 g speck or 3 rashers bacon
2–3 tablespoons olive oil
1 large onion, peeled and chopped
2 fat cloves garlic, crushed
1.5 kg chuck steak (best steak to use for long, slow cooking)
2 level tablespoons plain flour
½ cup (125 mL) water
1 stick celery, finely diced
1 large carrot, peeled and chopped into large dice
1½ cups (375 mL) dry red wine
2 tablespoons brandy
1 x 50 g sachet tomato paste
1 bay leaf
few sprigs fresh thyme or ½ level teaspoon dried thyme
1 level teaspoon salt, or to taste
freshly ground black pepper
pinch of ground nutmeg
375 g button or Swiss brown mushrooms, sliced
½ cup fresh parsley, chopped

Preheat oven to 130°–150°C (275°–300°F). Cut the speck or bacon into large dice, discarding the rind. Put into a saucepan, cover with cold water and bring slowly to the boil. Simmer for a few minutes then drain, rinse and pat dry. Heat gently in a large frying pan with 1 tablespoon of the oil, until the fat starts to sizzle, then add the onion and garlic. Sauté for five minutes, then transfer to a casserole dish.

Trim away any fat from the chuck steak, then cut into fairly large pieces and toss in the flour. Add the remaining oil to a frying pan and brown the meat in two or three batches. Transfer to the casserole dish. Rinse out the pan with the water, scraping with a wooden spoon to include all the crispy bits, then pour over the meat. Add the celery, carrot, wine, brandy, tomato paste, bay leaf and thyme.

Season with the salt, pepper and nutmeg. Push the meat down into the liquid, adding a little extra water if necessary so the meat is covered. Cover the dish with a lid and cook in the oven for about 2¼–2½ hours.

Sauté the mushrooms quickly in a little extra butter, then stir through the beef. Serve sprinkled with the parsley and accompanied by steaming hot boiled new potatoes and warm, crusty bread to mop up the luscious gravy. A green salad of mixed leaves with a garlicky dressing works well as an accompaniment or, alternatively, serve with boiled green peas.

To make the day before: Reduce the cooking time to about 2 hours (so meat doesn't overcook when reheated) and omit the mushrooms. Cool slightly (no longer than 30 minutes), then refrigerate immediately. Reheat in a slow oven (130°C/275°F) until well heated through, then stir in the freshly cooked mushrooms and sprinkle with the freshly chopped parsley. This casserole also freezes well — it will keep for up to 4 weeks. Thaw the frozen casserole in the refrigerator overnight, then reheat carefully.

My Mother's Meat Pie

Serves 6

I love the simple flavours in this pie and the way the pastry absorbs the meat juices so deliciously. The secret to success is the simplicity and the generous seasoning of black pepper.

2 rashers bacon, trimmed and chopped
1 level tablespoon butter
1 large onion, peeled and sliced
1.5 kg chuck steak, trimmed and chopped into small cubes
3 cups (750 mL) beef stock or water (if using packet stock, use half stock and half water)
1 stick celery, very finely chopped
few sprigs of fresh thyme or ½ teaspoon dried thyme
½ level teaspoon black pepper
½ level teaspoon salt
2 level tablespoons plain flour
a little milk or beaten egg
1 quantity Special Pie Pastry (see next page)

Cook the bacon in the butter in a large saucepan. When the fat starts to sizzle, add the onion. Sauté over a low heat for at least 5 minutes, or until the onion is soft and glossy (it is important to cook the onion well at this stage to develop a rich flavour — add a couple of teaspoons of water if necessary to keep the onion from burning). Add the chopped steak, stock, celery, thyme, pepper and salt. Cover the pot and simmer gently for about 1½ hours.

Preheat the oven to 220°C (425°F). Smooth out the flour with a little extra cold water, then stir this into the meat. Continue stirring over the heat until it boils and thickens. Taste, adding more salt and pepper if necessary, then pour into a deep pie dish. If you own a pie funnel, place in the centre of the meat (or substitute an upturned eggcup).

Roll out the pastry; cut a few strips for a collar. Place these on the wet rim of the pie dish and brush with milk or beaten egg. Lift remaining pastry onto a rolling pin and cover the pie. Trim the edges of the pastry with a knife. Press the edges together with a fork to seal and make a few steam holes. Glaze with beaten egg or milk and bake in the oven for 35–40 minutes. Serve with mashed potatoes and green peas ... and, for some Australians, meat pie just would not be complete without tomato sauce.

SPECIAL PIE PASTRY

Makes enough for one pie

This lovely old-fashioned pastry is especially good with meat pie.

¾ cup plain flour
¾ cup self-raising flour
100 g butter
3 tablespoons cold or ice water
1 teaspoon lemon juice

Place the flours and salt into a mixing bowl. Rub in the butter with your fingertips until the mixture resembles fine crumbs, then mix into a dough using the water and lemon juice. Turn out onto a lightly floured surface and knead lightly with a little extra flour. Rest the pastry for 20 minutes before rolling.

To make in food processor: Use chilled butter cut into small chunks. Place flours, salt and butter into food processor and process for a few seconds to cut into the butter. Add the water and juice, then process only long enough for the mixture to start to form a dough. Do not overmix. Turn out and knead lightly, and rest as above before rolling.

Italian Roast Chicken

Serves 4–6

This is a great dish for impromptu entertaining — just throw everything into a baking dish and forget about it while you make a salad.

2–3 tablespoons olive oil
6 chicken chops or thighs
6 chicken drumsticks
1 kg potatoes, peeled and cut into large golf-ball sized chunks
3 or 4 large cloves garlic, chopped
6 or 7 sprigs of fresh rosemary
chopped fresh parsley, to garnish

Preheat the oven to 200°C (400°F). Pour the olive oil into a large baking dish (one that will hold the chicken and potatoes in a single layer). Add the chicken and potatoes, and toss well to coat evenly with the oil, then add the garlic and rosemary. Bake in the oven for 50–60 minutes, or until the chicken and potatoes are cooked to a beautiful golden brown and the potatoes are crisp (if you like the potatoes extra crunchy, give them a little extra time after removing the chicken). Serve hot garnished with parsley and accompanied by a big salad of tossed mixed salad greens and sliced ripe tomatoes, and warm, crusty bread.

CRUMBED CHICKEN

Serves 4

I love the flavour of these juicy crumbed chicken pieces and there's a tantalising aroma in the kitchen while they're cooking.

8 chicken chops or thighs
1 cup soft white breadcrumbs
½ cup grated Parmesan cheese
2 tablespoons chopped fresh parsley
2 tablespoons chopped fresh chives
½ teaspoon dried thyme
1 teaspoon crushed garlic
1 teaspoon finely grated lemon rind
good pinch of salt
freshly ground black pepper
2 tablespoons olive oil
2 tablespoons melted butter

Preheat the oven to 200°C (400°F). Remove any excess fat from chicken. Combine the breadcrumbs, Parmesan cheese, parsley, chives, thyme, garlic and lemon rind. Season with salt and plenty of black pepper. Put the olive oil and butter into a small, shallow dish and spread the crumb mixture out onto a separate shallow tray. Dip the chicken pieces, one at a time, into the oil mixture, then coat with the breadcrumbs, firming the crumbs onto the chicken.

Arrange a single layer of the crumbed chicken in a large, shallow baking dish. Bake in the oven for 45 minutes, until chicken is cooked and the crust is golden and crisp. Don't turn the chicken over while it is cooking or the crumbs may fall off. Serve hot with a ripe tomato salad and young salad leaves.

Juicy Roast Tarragon Chicken

Serves 4

The chicken is very tender and juicy cooked this way and the juices in the baking dish make a delicious gravy. Cream sherry instead of the traditional white wine adds a richness of flavour and a subtle sweetness that works particularly well with chicken. My special thanks to Wendy Lungas from Con's Deli at Beecroft, NSW, for the idea. Wendy is an inspirational cook who is always generous with her ideas and recipes.

1 x large (1.6 kg) chicken
1 tablespoon softened butter
1 level teaspoon dried tarragon soaked in 1 tablespoon boiling water
¼ cup (65 mL) cream sherry or white wine
1 cup (250 mL) chicken stock
4 potatoes, peeled and halved
butter or oil, for roasting
3–4 ice cubes
1 level tablespoon butter
2 spring onions (white part only), very finely sliced
2 level teaspoons plain flour
salt and freshly ground black pepper, to taste
1 tablespoon finely chopped fresh chives

Preheat the oven to 190°C (375°F). Discard all excess fat from the chicken, then rub the softened butter into the skin. Put the chicken into a small baking dish (not too large as the juices will evaporate). Sprinkle the chicken evenly with the soaked tarragon, then add the sherry and ¼ cup of the chicken stock. Bake breast-side down in the oven for 30 minutes, then turn over and cook for a further 1–1¼ hours, basting often. Cover the breast with foil if it browns too much. Using a separate baking dish, roast potatoes in butter or oil for 1 hour.

Test the chicken to make sure it is cooked by piercing the legs with a fine skewer; the juices should run clear and show no signs of pink. The best place to test is where thigh joins the body; this always takes the longest time to cook. Remove the chicken from the oven and transfer to a hot plate; keep covered with foil while making the gravy.

Pour the juices from the baking dish into a large heatproof jug; add some ice cubes so that any fat rises to the surface for skimming. Melt the butter in the baking dish, then add the spring onion and cook gently for a minute. Sprinkle in the flour, then stir with a wooden spoon. Add the skimmed juices and the remaining chicken stock, then stir until boiling. Add extra water if necessary, season with salt and pepper to taste, then add the chives. Carve the chicken, then serve onto hot plates and spoon over the chicken gravy.

Mushroom Sauce: If you wish, you can add mushrooms to the chicken gravy. Slice 100 g firm button or Swiss brown mushrooms and sauté with the spring onion in the baking dish. Stir in the flour, then add the skimmed juices and the remaining chicken stock. Stir until boiling to make a delicious mushroom sauce.

THAI CHICKEN CURRY

Serves 4

Tender chicken and fresh vegetables cooked in a fragrant coconut broth.

6 chicken thigh fillets, fat removed
1 tablespoon light oil
1 small onion, peeled and chopped
1 large clove garlic, peeled and crushed
2 tablespoons finely grated fresh ginger
2–3 level tablepoons Australian-made Thai curry paste
1 cup (250 mL) water
1 kaffir lime leaf (fresh or dried)
270 mL coconut milk
250 g pumpkin, peeled and cut into thick slices
1 cup fresh, canned or frozen corn kernels
2 cups sliced button mushrooms
1 small red capsicum, finely sliced
2 small zucchini, sliced
1 tablespoon fish sauce (nam pla)
1 tablespoon fresh lime or lemon juice
salt, to taste
fresh coriander leaves, to garnish

Cut the chicken into large chunks. Put the oil in a wok with the onion, garlic and ginger, and stir-fry over a medium heat for a few minutes. Add the curry paste and cook for a minute or two longer. Add the chopped chicken, and toss in the fragrant spices until sealed but not browned, then add the water and kaffir lime leaf. Simmer the chicken gently for about 5 minutes, stirring occasionally to make sure it doesn't catch on the bottom. Add the coconut milk, pumpkin and corn, and cook for about 10 minutes longer, adding the mushrooms, capsicum and zucchini during the last few minutes or so. Add the fish sauce and lemon juice, and season with salt to taste. Serve hot with boiled jasmine rice. Garnish with the coriander leaves.

Note: If substituting imported curry pastes, reduce quantity to 1 level tablespoon (they're sometimes very hot), then taste and add more if you like.

Stir-fried Chicken & Noodles

Serves 4

Hokkien or Peking noodles with chicken and fresh vegetables in a slippery sauce.

500 g fresh Hokkien or Peking-style wheat noodles
1 tablespoon light vegetable oil
1 onion, peeled and cut into lengthwise strips
2 large cloves garlic, peeled and crushed
2 teaspoons grated fresh ginger
600 g chicken thigh fillets, trimmed of fat and cut into chunks
2 or 3 sticks celery
1 or 2 large red capsicums, sliced
1 cup (250 mL) water
150 g small zucchini, sliced
150 g mushrooms, sliced
2 tablespoons oyster sauce
1 tablespoon Ketjap Manis (Malaysian sweet soy sauce)
2 teaspoons sesame oil
dash of chilli sauce
chopped garlic chives or spring onion stems

Cook the noodles in a large saucepan of boiling, salted water for 2 minutes (5 minutes for Peking noodles), then drain.

While the noodles are cooking, put the oil into a wok with the onion, garlic and ginger. Stir-fry for a minute or two, taking care not to burn, then add the chicken and seal quickly, stirring often. Push the chicken up the sides of the wok, then add the celery and capsicum, and stir-fry briefly. Add the water and simmer for 5 minutes, until the chicken is cooked. Add the zucchini and mushrooms during last 2 minutes of cooking.

Add the drained noodles, oyster sauce, soy sauce, sesame oil and chilli sauce, then toss over a medium heat. Serve sprinkled with the chives or spring onions.

Note: As an alternative, char-grill the capsicum separately (see page 76) to remove the skin. Serve the noodles in the bowl, with big succulent chunks of capsicum on top, and finish with bright green, chopped spring onion.

Chicken Pie

Serves 6

A gorgeous old-fashioned pie to tuck into on a cold, wintry night.

1 large (1.8 kg) chicken
good pinch of salt
a few black peppercorns
1 bay leaf
2–3 spring onions, chopped
strip of lemon peel
several ice cubes
3 medium carrots, peeled and diced
1 parsnip, peeled and diced
2 sticks celery, diced
2 level tablespoons short-grain rice
50 g butter
1 onion, peeled and sliced
2 level tablespoons plain flour
2 heaped tablespoons crème fraiche or cream (optional)
2 tablespoons chopped fresh parsley
2 tablespoons chopped fresh chives
¼ level teaspoon dried thyme
salt and freshly ground black pepper, to taste
375 g packet puff pastry or use ready-rolled puff pastry sheets
1 egg, beaten and mixed with 1 tablespoon milk, to glaze the pie

Put the chicken into a large saucepan and cover with water. Add the salt, peppercorns, bay leaf, spring onion and lemon peel. Simmer until cooked, about 1 hour. Remove the chicken from the stock as soon as it is cooked and refrigerate until it's cool enough to handle. When cool, discard any skin and bones, and cut the chicken into chunks, then cover and refrigerate. Strain the stock into a bowl, add several ice cubes, then skim away any fat that rises to the surface. Refrigerate 3 cups (750 mL) of this stock for the sauce.

Put the remaining stock into a saucepan with the carrots, parsnip and celery, and bring to the boil. Add the rice and simmer for 10 minutes, then strain.

Meanwhile, melt the butter in a large saucepan and sauté the onion until soft. Stir in the flour to make a roux, then add the reserved 3 cups stock and stir until the sauce boils and thickens. Add the chopped chicken, then add the strained vegetables and rice. Stir to mix through the smooth chicken sauce. Enrich with crème fraiche (if using). Add the parsley, chives and thyme, and season to taste with salt and pepper.

Reheat the oven to 220°C (425°F). Transfer the chicken filling to a 22 cm pie plate or 6 individual ramekins. Roll out the pastry and cut it a little larger than the top of the pie. Let the pastry stand for 10 minutes (this prevents it shrinking in the oven), then place over the filling. Seal to the edges of the dish with a little egg glaze. Glaze the pastry with the egg mixture, then make a few steam holes. Bake in the oven until the pastry is well risen and crisp and golden, about 35 minutes.

Note: If making one large pie in a pie plate, cut a thin strip of pastry and place on wetted rim of the plate to form a collar. Glaze this with egg, *then* cover with the pastry lid and seal pastry edges with a fork.

Greek Roast Lamb with Lemon

Serves 6

1 x 2 kg leg of lamb
2–3 large cloves garlic, peeled and slivered
salt and freshly ground black pepper
6 medium potatoes (Pontiac or Desirée)
1 tablespoon olive oil
4 tablespoons fresh lemon juice
¾ cup water
1 level teaspoon dried oregano or rigani (Greek oregano)

Preheat the oven to 200°–220°C (400°–425°F). Trim and discard any excess fat from lamb then, using the tip of a small vegetable knife, make deep slits in the meat and insert the slivers of garlic. Season the lamb with salt and a generous quantity of black pepper, then put into a large baking dish. Cook, uncovered, in the oven for 45 minutes or until the meat starts to brown.

Meanwhile, wash the potatoes but do not peel. Cut each one in half, then toss in the olive oil. Mix the lemon juice and water together in a small dish and reserve. Remove the baking dish from oven using an oven cloth to protect your hands, then arrange the potatoes around the meat. Pour the lemon juice mixture evenly over the lamb, then sprinkle meat and potatoes with the oregano. Cover the baking dish with foil, sealing at the edges, then bake for a further 45–60 minutes (allow slightly longer if you prefer the lamb to be well done).

When cooked, remove the lamb and potatoes from the baking dish and keep covered while preparing the gravy. Pour the juices from the baking dish into a jug, then add a handful of ice cubes so any fat will rise to the top. Skim away all the excess fat, then reheat the gravy and dilute with water if necessary.

Serve this delicious lemon gravy with the carved meat and herbed potatoes. Accompany with sweet young green peas and warm, crusty bread to mop up all the delicious juices.

Note: If you prefer lightly thickened gravy, mix 1 level tablespoon plain flour with the lemon juice and water. This will thicken the lemon gravy in the dish as the lamb cooks.

Irish Stew

Serves 4–6

There are times when the comforting and gentle flavour of this lamb stew is just what the doctor ordered. But in these health-conscious days, rather than cooking the chops whole, it makes good sense to eliminate the fat from the meat before cooking.

1–1.5 kg best neck lamb chops
4 or 5 large potatoes (750 g–1 kg)
1 large onion, peeled and sliced
1 or 2 leeks, trimmed, washed and sliced
6 sprigs fresh thyme or ½ teaspoon dried thyme
½ teaspoon salt
freshly ground black pepper, to taste
chopped fresh parsley, to garnish

Chop the meat into chunks, discarding all the fat. Put the lamb bones into a saucepan and cover well with water. Cover the pan loosely with a lid and simmer for about 45 minutes. When ready, strain stock, discarding bones. Put aside.

Peel the potatoes, then slice one and cut remainder into quarters. Put layers of potato, onion, leek and lamb into a large, heavy-based saucepan. Tuck in the thyme sprigs, then pour over the strained lamb stock. Top up with more water if necessary so that all the ingredients are covered with liquid. Add the salt, then cover the pot and lower the heat. Simmer for about 1 hour, or until the meat is tender. Stir the pan now and then to make sure it doesn't catch on the bottom, adding more water or stock if necessary. The sliced potato should break up into the stew creating a light thickening.

Season with black pepper to taste and a little extra salt if necessary. Serve sprinkled generously with chopped parsley and accompany with boiled green peas and fresh bread and butter.

Note: As with most stews, this dish is even better the next day. Store any leftovers in the refrigerator immediately. Reheat in the microwave or alternatively in a saucepan over a low heat, adding a little extra liquid if necessary.

LAMB CURRY

Serves 6

When it has to be a lamb curry, try this delicious recipe my friend Ruki shared with me one memorable day in her kitchen. Ruki cooked while a group of passionate foodies took copious notes.

1 x 2 kg leg of lamb
1 tablespoon fresh lemon juice
½ level teaspoon black pepper
2 large onions, peeled and chopped
2 level tablespoons ghee or butter, plus a little extra
2 level teaspoons grated fresh ginger
2 cloves garlic, peeled and crushed
2 level tablespoons curry powder
1 level teaspoon cardamom seeds, crushed
¼ teaspoon ground cloves
½ teaspoon ground chillies
1 stick cinnamon
2 sprigs of curry leaves (see Note)
3 ripe tomatoes, chopped
1 x 280 mL can of coconut milk
1½ cups (375 mL) water
strip of fresh lemon peel
4 level tablespoons desiccated coconut, dry-toasted until golden
1 level teaspoon salt
few sprigs of fresh coriander
few sprigs of mint

Cut the lamb into large chunks, discarding as much of the fat as possible. Place in a bowl, then add the lemon juice and pepper, and mix well. Cover and refrigerate for 1 hour or overnight.

Cook the onion in 1 level tablespoon of the ghee in a large saucepan over a low heat, until glossy and just tinged with gold (keep an eye on it as onions can burn easily). Puree the cooked onion in a food processor to make a paste (see following).

Heat the remaining ghee in the same saucepan as used to cook the onion, then add the ginger, garlic and curry powder. Cook very gently, stirring with a wooden spoon, for a minute or so. Add the cardamom seeds, ground cloves, chillies, cinnamon and curry leaves. Add a little more ghee, then add the lamb and fry until sealed, stirring often to coat the fragrant mixture.

Add the tomatoes, coconut milk and water. Return the onion paste to the curry, then add the lemon peel, coconut and salt. Add the coriander and mint, then cover the pan and simmer gently for 1–1½ hours, adding extra water if necessary.

This curry is best if made a day ahead; store in the refrigerator until needed. Remove any excess ghee from the surface, then gently reheat the curry. Serve with basmati rice, pappadams and the usual accompaniments.

Note: Curry leaves are added to a curry in much the same way as bay leaves are added to a stew in Western cooking. They are available fresh and dried from Asian food stores and markets. Curry leaf trees are often available from Asian markets or Indian spice shops and make an attractive addition to the herb garden.

Onion Puree: Making a paste of the cooked onions does make a subtle difference to this curry, but if you don't own a food processor or you are in a hurry, simply omit this step.

BAKED DINNER

Serves 6

When far away from home, many Australians yearn for lamb roast with pumpkin, potatoes and gravy, and it's often the first thing we request on our return. A baked dinner is one of the easiest things to cook, but some new cooks complain that it is a bit tricky at the last minute, with the meat to carve, getting the vegetables just right and gravy to make ... here are tips for success.

1 large leg of lamb (about 2 kg)
salt and freshly ground black pepper, to taste
750 g potatoes
750 g pumpkin (choose good dry pumpkin or kumara)

Preheat the oven to 200°C (400°F). Season the lamb with salt and pepper, then put into a large baking dish. Bake in the oven for about 1½ hours (more or less according to taste). Peel the potatoes and cut into halves. Par-boil for 5 minutes, drain immediately into a colander, then place around the roast with chunks of peeled pumpkin or kumara during the last 40 minutes of cooking.

When the lamb is cooked, remove from the baking dish and let stand in a warm spot for 5 minutes before carving. Transfer the potatoes, pumpkin and all the fat from the baking dish into a large shallow slab tin, saving the precious meat sediment in the baking dish for the gravy. Increase the oven temperature to 230°C (450°F) and return the vegetables to the oven.

Put accompanying vegetables such as peas or beans on to boil. Meanwhile, enlist some help to carve the meat while you make the gravy, then serve the carved meat on hot plates, moistened with a little gravy. Add the vegetables and accompany with Mint Sauce.

Gravy: Add about 1 cup (250 mL) water to the meat sediment in the baking dish then simmer for a few minutes to make a delicious unthickened gravy. Season to taste with salt and freshly ground black pepper. If you like a thickened gravy, add 2 slightly heaped teaspoons gravy mix (blended first with a little water). Stir constantly with a wooden spoon until thickened, then thin down with extra water (don't make the mistake of having gravy too thick — keep the consistency light).

Mint Sauce

¼ cup fresh mint leaves, finely chopped
1 tablespoon boiling water
3 tablespoons brown malt vinegar
1½ level tablespoons sugar
pinch of salt
freshly ground black pepper, to taste

Put the mint in a small heatproof jug. Pour over the boiling water to set the colour, then add the vinegar, sugar, salt and pepper, and stir well. Let stand for at least 30 minutes for the flavours to mingle and soften before using.

Lamb Chop and Potato Bake

Serves 4–6

This is a comforting family dish with gentle flavours that everyone seems to like. The inclusion of the apple provides a natural sweetness, and fresh mint adds a burst of fresh flavour.

6 large lamb forequarter or leg chops, trimmed of fat
salt and freshly ground black pepper, to taste
1 level tablespoon plain flour
6 medium potatoes (1 kg), peeled and thinly sliced
1 large onion, peeled and thinly sliced
1 level tablespoon brown sugar
2 tablespoons brown malt vinegar
3 cooking apples, peeled and cored
2 teaspoons melted butter or oil
2 tablespoons chopped fresh parsley
3 large sprigs fresh mint, chopped

Preheat the oven to 200°C (450°F). Season the chops with salt and black pepper, then dust both sides lightly with flour. Spread two-thirds of the potatoes over the base of a greased baking dish. Scatter the onion over the potatoes then add a layer of the floured lamb chops. Sprinkle the vinegar and the brown sugar over this and add the sliced apples. Pour over just enough boiling water to barely cover the chops. Arrange the remaining sliced potato in an even layer over the top, then brush with a little melted butter or oil. Cover the dish with a sheet of greased foil (with greased side next to potato so it doesn't stick).

Bake in the oven for 2 hours, removing the foil for the last 20 minutes so the potato topping can brown slightly.

Serve the chops, potatoes, cooked apples and gravy sprinkled with a generous quantity of chopped parsley and mint. Accompany with sweet young green peas and some thin slices fresh bread and butter to mop up the delicious gravy.

SHEPHERD'S PIE

Serves 4

There's a secret to this pie's crisp potato topping, which you will discover when you read the recipe.

4 or 5 medium potatoes (750 g), peeled and cut into chunks
leftover roast lamb, sufficient for 2–3 cups when minced
1 onion, peeled and thinly sliced
1 level tablespoon butter, plus extra for topping
1 medium carrot, coarsely grated
¼ cup very finely diced celery
1 ripe tomato, finely chopped
few sprigs of fresh parsley, chopped
1 teaspoon Worcestershire sauce
3 level tablespoons tomato sauce
freshly ground black pepper, to taste
tiny pinch of salt
2 tablespoons water

Boil the potatoes in salted water in a covered saucepan until tender, about 20 minutes. While the potatoes are cooking, mince the lamb in a food processor or mincer (or chop very finely with a sharp knife), then transfer to a mixing bowl. Cook the onion in the butter in a small frying pan until soft and glossy, then add to the lamb with the carrot, celery, tomato and parsley. Mix well, then season with the Worcestershire sauce, tomato sauce and black pepper to taste. Add the salt and moisten the mixture with the water (the mixture should be moist, but not wet). Preheat the oven to 220°C (425°C).

Drain and mash the potatoes, adding about 1 tablespoon soft butter, then season with salt and pepper to taste (don't be tempted to add milk — the potato should be fairly dry to ensure a crisp topping). Spread the lamb mixture into a shallow, well-greased pie plate, then pile on potato and spread to the edges, roughing the surface into peaks with a fork. Brush with extra melted butter (or add a few dots of butter on the potato here and there). Bake in the hottest part of the oven for about 40 minutes, until steaming hot and the topping is golden.

Savoury Mince

Serves 4–6

The flavour of this dish improves if refrigerated overnight. Any leftovers are great on toast then smothered with chopped parsley.

1 large onion, peeled and sliced
1 tablespoon butter or oil
1 large clove garlic, crushed (optional)
500–750 g best minced steak
1 large carrot, peeled and diced
2 sticks celery, diced
1 parsnip or small turnip, peeled and finely diced
1 large ripe tomato, chopped
1 tablespoon Worcestershire sauce or soy sauce
2 tablespoons tomato sauce or 1 tablespoon tomato paste
pinch of dried thyme
good pinch of salt
1 beef or chicken stock cube (optional)
1 cup (250 mL) water
freshly ground black pepper, to taste
2 level teaspoons plain flour
squeeze of lemon juice
2 tablespoons chopped fresh parsley

Put the onion, butter and garlic (if using) into a large saucepan or wok. Cook over a medium heat until the onion is soft. Increase the heat and add the minced steak and stir-fry until the meat changes colour. Drain off and discard any fat that may have accumulated in the pan. Add the carrot, celery, parsnip and tomato. Stir through, then add the Worcestershire sauce, tomato sauce, thyme and salt. Crumble in the stock cube (if using), then add the water. Season generously with black pepper, then cover the pan and simmer for about 15 minutes. Add extra water if necessary. Mix the flour with a little water, then add to the mince and stir until it is slightly thickened (this keeps the mince moist). Add a good squeeze of lemon juice to sharpen the flavour, then serve sprinkled with parsley. Serve with either plain, boiled potatoes or mashed potatoes, and green beans.

Spaghetti Bolognaise

Serves 6–8

Meat Sauce
1 large or 2 medium onions, peeled and chopped
2 tablespoons oil
2 large cloves garlic, finely chopped
750 g minced steak
1 level teaspoon dried oregano
1 level teaspoon dried thyme
1 bay leaf
1 cup (250 mL) white wine
1½ cups (375 mL) water
2 x 425 g cans peeled tomatoes
2 x 50 g sachets tomato paste
½ level teaspoon salt
freshly ground black pepper
200 g mushrooms, sliced

To Serve
500–750 g dried spaghetti or bucatini (100 g per adult serve)
torn fresh basil leaves or chopped fresh parsley
grated or shaved Parmesan cheese

Put the onion, oil and garlic into large saucepan then cook very gently, stirring often, for 5 minutes, until the onion is soft and glossy. Add the minced steak and stir often until lightly browned, then add the oregano, thyme, bay leaf, wine, water, tomatoes and tomato paste. Add the salt and a generous quantity of black pepper. Simmer gently for 1 hour, adding extra water as necessary. Add the mushrooms to the meat sauce during the last 10 minutes of cooking.

This sauce is best made the day before and refrigerated. Before reheating, remove all the excess fat from the top of the sauce, then reheat and adjust consistency. Serve over freshly cooked pasta and sprinkle with basil leaves or parsley, and Parmesan cheese. Any leftover meat sauce is good reheated on toast.

Easy Lasagne

Serves 6–8

Lasagne freezes beautifully and is one of the great comfort foods. Keep a batch in the freezer for emergencies (guaranteed not to stay there too long).

1 50 g sachet tomato paste
1 cup boiling water
4 cups cooked meat sauce, mushrooms optional (see Spaghetti Bolognaise page 61)
200 g instant frilly lasagne noodles (no pre-cooking required)
Béchamel Sauce (see recipe following)
200 g mozzarella cheese, sliced
2 tablespoons grated Parmesan cheese

Preheat the oven to 200°C (400°F). Mix tomato paste with boiling water, then add to the meat sauce. Brush a shallow oblong ovenproof dish with olive oil, then put a layer of the meat sauce on the bottom. Add a layer of lasagne noodles, then a layer of the béchamel sauce. Add another layer of meat sauce, then some sliced mozzarella. Add more lasagne noodles and continue with remaining ingredients until the dish is filled, finishing with a layer of béchamel. Sprinkle with the Parmesan and bake in the oven for about 30 minutes. Cut into 6 or 8 portions and serve hot with a big green salad tossed with garlicky vinaigrette.

Béchamel Sauce (with cheese)

50 g butter
4 level tablespoons plain flour
3½ cups (875 mL) milk
salt, freshly ground black pepper, and a little ground nutmeg
1 cup grated tasty cheddar cheese

Melt the butter in a saucepan. Stir in the flour to make a roux, cook for a few minutes, then remove from the heat and stir in the milk. Return to the heat and stir constantly until the sauce boils and thickens. Beat well until smooth and shiny. Season with salt, pepper and nutmeg to taste, then stir in the grated cheese.

Margaret's Meat Balls in Tomato Sauce

Serves 6

Tomato Sauce
1 tablespoon olive oil
1 onion, peeled and chopped
2 large cloves garlic, crushed
1 chilli, finely chopped (optional)
500 or 600 mL jar tomato cooking sauce
½ cup (125 mL) white wine
½ level teaspoon dried oregano
2 cups (500 mL) water

Meat Balls
500 g best lean minced beef
2 cups soft breadcrumbs
½ cup chopped fresh parsley
½ cup grated Parmesan cheese
2 cloves garlic, crushed
1 egg
salt and freshly ground black pepper, to taste

To make the tomato sauce, put the olive oil into a large saucepan with the onion, garlic and chilli. Cook over a low heat for 5 minutes. Add tomato sauce, wine, oregano and water. Simmer the sauce for 30 minutes.

To make the meat balls, put the mince in a large mixing bowl, then add the breadcrumbs, parsley, Parmesan, garlic and egg. Season with salt and pepper to taste. Combine thoroughly, kneading with the heel of your hand for a minute. Roll the mixture into 3 cm balls (no bigger than this, they swell during cooking).

Heat a little olive oil in a large frying pan, fry a batch of meatballs until sealed, then remove to drain on paper towels. Fry the rest in batches, then add them to the simmering tomato sauce. Simmer very gently for 10 minutes. Serve hot with pasta and grated Parmesan cheese.

Pork Sausages in Tomato and Cumin Gravy

Serves 4

8 lean pork sausages (from a good butcher)
1 level tablespoon butter
1 small onion, peeled and sliced
1 teaspoon grated fresh ginger
1 clove garlic, peeled and crushed
2 level teaspoons ground cumin
2 level teaspoons plain flour
1–1½ cups (250–375 mL) water
500 g ripe tomatoes (3 medium), halved
1 teaspoon sugar
salt and freshly ground black pepper, to taste
fresh coriander leaves or chopped parsley, to garnish

Fry the sausages in the butter until cooked, then transfer from the frying pan onto a plate. Pour off all but 1 tablespoon of fat from the pan, add the onion and cook gently for 5 minutes, then add the ginger, garlic and cumin. Cook for a minute longer, then stir in the flour and let it brown slightly. Add water then grate in the tomatoes, discarding the skin. Add the sugar and salt and pepper to taste. Simmer the sauce for about 5 minutes, then return the sausages to the pan. Allow them to cook gently in the sauce for a few minutes, or until the sauce has reduced to a good consistency. Serve sprinkled with coriander or parsley, and accompany with mashed potatoes and one green vegetable.

Pork in Satay Sauce

Serves 4

750 g tender pork (use 2 pork fillets or pork neck, also known as Scotch fillet of pork)
1 clove garlic, peeled and crushed
1 teaspoon grated fresh ginger
2 tablespoons light vegetable oil
1 tablespoon sesame oil
2 level teasppons ground cumin
1 level teaspoon ground coriander
½ level teaspoon ground turmeric
1 lemon
1 onion, peeled and sliced into slivers (from stem to base)
1 level tablespoon Jimmy's Satay Sauce
1 level tablespooon peanut butter (crunchy or smooth)
1 level tablespoon brown sugar
¼ cup fresh coriander leaves
few sprigs of fresh mint

Discard any fat from the pork, then cut the meat into 1 cm thick slices. If using pork neck, cut each slice into four. Put the meat into a bowl, then add the garlic, ginger, 1 tablespoon vegetable oil, sesame oil, cumin, coriander and turmeric. Pare a thin strip of peel from the lemon and add to the meat, then stir well. Cover and marinate in the refrigerator for at least 30 minutes or, if you prefer, overnight.

Put the onion into a small saucepan, cover with water and simmer for 5 minutes, then drain well. Place the onion in a wok or saucepan with the remaining tablespoon of vegetable oil and cook gently for a few minutes. Add all the marinated meat, oil and spices from the bowl. Reserve the lemon peel. Stir-fry until the meat is sealed, then add 1 cup (250 mL) water, satay sauce, peanut butter, brown sugar, 2 tablespoons fresh lemon juice and reserved lemon peel. Simmer until the sauce thickens and the meat is tender (add a little extra water or white wine if necessary). Add the coriander leaves during the last few minutes.

Season with salt if necessary, then remove the peel. Serve in a shallow bowl with the fresh mint scattered over the top. This dish is good with plain boiled rice and butter lettuce.

Roast Pork with Crackling

Serves 6–8

If you love the crackling (and who doesn't) consider cooking a pork rack.

---

1 rack (loin) of pork
kitchen salt
1 tablespoon oil
6–8 medium potatoes

There's extra crackling on this roast because the rib bones are not trimmed. When ordering from the butcher, ask for it to be prepared for easy carving (removing chine bone and cut through the bones at the base) and with the rind scored.

Preheat the oven to 200°–210°C (400°–425°F). Rub the rind of the pork with kitchen salt then put the roast into a baking dish with the oil. Bake in the oven for about 1¼–1½ hours (depending on the size of the rack), increasing to 230°–250°C (425°–500°F) during the last 30 minutes to pop the crackling. Try not to overcook the meat; it is best when it is nice and juicy. To carve the rack, simply cut through the cutlets as you would a rack of lamb. Roast potatoes should be added during the last hour of cooking.

Gravy: Remove meat and potatoes to a warm plate. Pour away all but 1 tablespoon of the fat in the baking dish. Put the baking dish over a low heat on cooktop, then sprinkle in 1 tablespoon plain flour. Stir briefly with a wooden spoon, then gradually add sufficient water to make a thin gravy. Stir constantly until the gravy thickens. Season with freshly ground black pepper.

Standing Pork Roast is the pork rack (or loin) with the bones trimmed. The chine bone is completely removed, leaving only the rib bones attached to the loin. The roast is then tied to hold its shape. There is less crackling than the rack, but the roast is easy to carve into slices. Cooking time and method is the same as the pork rack.

Leg of Pork: Rub the scored skin with salt. Allow 30 minutes cooking time for each 500 g of pork. Cooking time is longer than for the loin, so use a slightly lower heat 180°–190°C (350°–375°F) so the fat doesn't burn, then increase the heat to 260°C (500°F) (allow 10°C less for fan-forced ovens) during the last 45 minutes to pop the crackling and crisp the potatoes.

Crackling: To make the crackling on the pork, it's necessary to increase the oven temperature to full blast at least 30 minutes before the end of the cooking time. Some very good cooks favour a very hot oven to start, then finish the cooking at a lower heat. I've had more success by cooking the pork in a hot oven (200°–210°C/400°–425°F) to start, then increasing to full blast 260°C (500°F) for the last 30 minutes or so to pop the crackling.

The crackling didn't work? Don't panic, simply remove the skin, cut into strips and deep-fry in hot oil.

Pork Neck (Scotch Fillet of Pork)

Serves 6–8

A juicy and tender pork roast with absolutely no waste.

olive oil
1.25 to 1.5 kg pork neck

Preheat the oven to 190°C (375°F). Rub a little olive oil over the pork, then place the meat in a baking dish with 1 tablespoon olive oil. Roast in the oven for 1¼–1½ hours. Test with a skewer to see if the pork is cooked (when cooked, the juices will run clear). Remove from the oven, cover with foil and let stand in a warm place to 'rest' for 10 minutes. Cut into slices and serve hot with a suitable sauce or cold with salads.

Veal Casserole

Serves 6–8

Tender veal is cooked with fresh tomatoes, white wine and herbs.

1.5 kg veal shoulder
2 level tablespoons plain flour
50 g butter, plus 1 tablespoon extra
1 cup (250 mL) water
1 cup (250 mL) white wine
2 rashers bacon, trimmed and chopped
2 medium onions, peeled and sliced
600 g ripe tomatoes (3 large), peeled and chopped
1 level teaspoon dried rosemary
½ teaspoon dried thyme
1 level tablespoon finely chopped fresh garlic
1 level teaspoon salt, to taste
¼ teaspoon black pepper
chopped fresh parsley

Preheat the oven to 180°C (350°F). Cut the veal into large cubes, toss in the flour, then brown lightly in the 50 g butter in a large frying pan (do this in batches). Transfer the veal to a casserole dish. Add the water to the frying pan and stir to include all the crusty pan juices, then add this to the casserole along with the white wine.

Cook the bacon in a clean pan until the fat sizzles, then move to one side of pan. Add the extra 1 tablespoon of butter and sauté the onions until they are soft. Add to the veal in the casserole with the tomatoes, rosemary, thyme, garlic, salt and pepper. Cover, then bake in the oven for about 1 hour (don't overcook or the meat will fall apart).

Serve sprinkled generously with parsley and accompany with mashed potatoes and sweet young green peas.

Veal and Mushroom Stew

Serves 6

Veal is simmered with wine, mustard and mushrooms and finished with a dash of cream.

1 large onion, peeled and sliced
50 g butter
1 kg veal shoulder steak, trimmed and chopped
2 level teaspoons mustard powder
2 level tablespoons plain flour
1 cup dry white wine
3 cups (750 mL) water
½ level teaspoon salt
freshly ground black pepper, to taste
500 g large flat mushrooms (use button mushrooms if flats are not available), sliced
4 tablespoons cream
juice of ¼ lemon
parsley, to garnish
chives, to garnish
dill, to garnish

Put the onion and butter into a heavy-based saucepan or flameproof casserole dish and cook gently for about 5 minutes. Increase the heat, then add the veal and fry, stirring frequently until well sealed and lightly browned. Sprinkle over the mustard and flour, then stir through the meat. Add the white wine and water and bring to the boil, stirring occasionally, then add the salt and pepper. Cover the stew, lower the heat and simmer very gently for about 40 minutes or until the veal is tender. Stir in the mushrooms and cream and simmer for a further 5–10 minutes, adding a dash more wine or water if necessary. Just before serving, finish with a tiny squeeze lemon juice.

Serve garnished with chopped fresh herbs, and accompany with fluffy mashed potato or boiled fettuccine noodles and sweet young green peas.

Pot Roast of Veal with Mushroom Sauce

Serves 6–8

1 x 2 kg boned rolled and tied shoulder of veal
2 level tablespoons butter
1 large onion, peeled and sliced
1 clove garlic, peeled and crushed
few sprigs fresh thyme or ½ teaspoon dried thyme
freshly ground black pepper, to taste
1½ cups (375 mL) white wine
400 g button or Swiss brown mushrooms, sliced
1 level tablespoon plain flour
1 heaped tablespoon thick sour cream
1 heaped teaspoon smooth French or German mustard
chopped chives, parsley or dill, to garnish

Preheat the oven to 180°C (350°F). Brown the veal slowly in the butter in a frying pan, adding the onion halfway through browning. Transfer the meat and onion to a large casserole dish. Add the garlic, thyme, black pepper to taste and wine. Cover the dish and bake in the oven for 1½–2 hours. Remove the meat from the casserole and keep warm, then enlist some help to slice the meat while preparing the sauce.

Sauté the mushrooms in a little extra butter in a pan, then sprinkle with the flour. Add the liquid from the casserole and simmer for 5 minutes or so. Add the sour cream and mustard, and heat gently. Serve the sliced meat with the mushroom sauce and sprinkle with chives, parsley or dill. Accompany with plain boiled potatoes or buttered noodles, and one green vegetable (spinach or asparagus would be a good choice).

Note: The veal shoulder is exceptionally tender and juicy, but it contains some white gristle which, if not removed, could spoil the dish. Make sure the butcher removes this before rolling the meat.

Vegetables and Salads

Layered Avocado Salad
Basil Pesto with Pasta
Bean and Potato Salad
Spiced Chickpea Salad
Grilled Capsicum
Moroccan Carrots
Glazed Tarragon Carrots
Carrot and Potato Fritters
Cauliflower Cheese
Mini Corn Flapjacks
Sam's Baked Eggplant
Caponata
Couscous
Mushrooms on Toast
Soft Polenta with Mushrooms and tomatoes
Mashed Potato
Potato and Celeriac Mash
Olive Oil Mash
Potato Gratin
Farmer's Potato Bake
Coriander Potatoes in Fresh Tomato Sauce
Creamy Potato Salad
Favourite Green Salad
Turkish Pilaf Rice
Shepherd's Salad
Tomato and Basil Salad

Layered Avocado Salad

Serves 4

This is a good salad to serve for a light lunch accompanied by warm, crusty bread.

1 iceberg or cos lettuce (or 2 butterhead lettuces), washed and separated into leaves
1 stick celery (use tender inside portion), thinly sliced
2 firm, vine-ripened tomatoes, chopped
2 avocados, peeled and cut into thick slices
2 tablespoons olive oil
2 teaspoons fresh lemon juice
2 teaspoons balsamic vinegar
1 clove garlic, crushed
3–4 spring onions, trimmed and sliced
4 bacon rashers, trimmed of fat, freshly cooked and chopped

Tear the lettuce leaves and store in a crisper until ready to use. Just before serving, place a layer of the torn lettuce leaves into a shallow salad bowl, then add layers of the celery, tomato and avocado. Make a dressing with the oil; lemon juice, balsamic vinegar and garlic, then drizzle over the salad. Sprinkle the salad with the spring onions and bacon. Serve with warm crusty bread.

Note: Spring onions are known as shallots or green onions in New South Wales.

Basil Pesto with Pasta

Serves 4

A great comfort food in summer when basil is at its best.

½ cup tightly packed fresh basil leaves
1–2 large cloves garlic, chopped
1 slightly rounded tablespoon pine nuts
4 tablespoons olive oil
½ cup freshly grated Parmesan cheese
250 g dried fettuccine, spaghetti or penne

Put the basil leaves, chopped garlic and pine nuts into a food processor bowl. Process until finely chopped then, with the machine still going, gradually add the oil (drop by drop at first, just as you do when making mayonnaise) until a smooth paste is formed. Add the Parmesan and process again briefly. Transfer the pesto to a small basin and cover immediately (right down onto the surface) with plastic wrap to retain the green colour.

Cook the pasta in plenty of boiling, salted water until al dente. Cooking time depends on the type of pasta used. Taste a few strands to check if it's done; try not to overcook.

Meanwhile, heat a large serving bowl and the pasta plates (cooked pasta cools quickly). Drain the pasta, reserving a little of the cooking water. Put the pasta into the hot bowl. Add a couple of tablespoons of the reserved cooking water to the pesto sauce, then pour the sauce over the drained pasta and toss quickly. Serve immediately, accompanied with warm Italian bread and a crisp green salad.

Note: If tightly sealed to exclude air, pesto will keep in the refrigerator for a day or two. Once the surface is exposed to the air, the colour will darken. If you need to make it ahead, try adding some flat-leaf parsley with the basil. The parsley intensifies the green colour.

Bean and Potato Salad

Serves 8

The fresh lemon dressing works particularly well in this salad. Serve as an accompaniment to barbecued meats, fish or poultry.

500 g Desirée potatoes (or use Pontiac or Petrone), washed and cut into large chunks (do not peel)
juice of ½ lemon
250 g fresh green beans (use stringless baby beans or Italian flat beans, stringed)
1 x 400 g can borlotti beans
1 small Spanish onion, peeled and very finely sliced
300 g firmly-ripe egg tomatoes, diced
2 tablespoons chopped fresh parsley
½ level teaspoon dried oregano
salt and freshly ground black pepper, to taste

Lemon Dressing
2 tablespoons extra virgin olive oil
1 tablespoon fresh lemon juice
1 teaspoon white or red wine vinegar (or use balsamic vinegar)
1 level teaspoon finely grated lemon rind
1 clove garlic, peeled and crushed

Cook the potatoes in boiling salted water with a good squeeze of lemon juice in a covered saucepan for about 15 minutes or until tender, but still holding their shape. Drain and cool. String the beans (if necessary) and cut into 5 cm lengths (if using baby beans, leave them whole). Blanch the beans briefly in a saucepan of boiling salted water for 3–5 minutes, until crispy-tender but still bright green, then refresh in cold water (to stop further cooking) and drain. Drain the borlotti beans and put into a salad bowl with the potatoes, green beans, onion and tomato. Add the parsley and oregano and season with salt and pepper to taste. Chill until ready to serve.

To make the Lemon Dressing, combine the oil, lemon juice, vinegar, lemon rind and garlic in a small bottle. Shake well, then pour over salad just before serving.

SPICED CHICKPEA SALAD

Serves 6–8

This is a good picnic salad because it carries well. It is delicious as an accompaniment to fish, chicken or lamb or spooned into pocket bread with lettuce and chopped tomatoes.

2 tablespoons olive oil
1 onion, peeled and chopped
2 cloves garlic, crushed
1 fresh chilli, seeds discarded then finely chopped
1–1½ level teaspoons ground cumin
½ level teaspoon ground coriander
½ level teaspoon garam masala
2 x 300 g cans chickpeas, drained
rind of 1 lemon, grated
1 tablespoon fresh lemon juice
fresh coriander, chopped
parsley leaves, chopped

Put the olive oil and onion into a small frying pan and cook over a very gentle heat, stirring frequently with a wooden spoon until the onion is soft and glossy and just starting to turn golden. Add the garlic, chilli, cumin, ground coriander and garam masala and cook a minute longer. Remove from the heat and transfer the onion and spice mixture (including all the oil from the pan) to a mixing bowl. Add the chickpeas, toss the mixture well, then stir in the lemon rind, lemon juice, fresh coriander and parsley.

Grilled Capsicum

Capsicums are succulent and juicy when prepared this way.

Large red or yellow capsicums are the best ones to use. Cut into quarters, discard seeds then cook *skin side up* under a griller until the skin blackens and blisters. (Alternatively, cook *skin side down* in an oiled pan or on a barbecue hotplate.)

To remove skins, plunge the capsicums immediately into a bowl of cold water. Alternatively, let them cool for a minute then put them into a plastic bag to steam. Leave for 5 minutes or so, then peel away the blackened skin. Cut the capsicum into slivers or wide strips and put into a dish. Drizzle over a little olive oil, then add a squeeze lemon juice and a few drops of balsamic vinegar. They are good with grilled lamb or veal chops, or with barbecued steaks.

To make a capsicum relish, add a few capers, a little crushed garlic and some fresh marjoram leaves. Serve as an antipasto or with thick, barbecued fish steaks. Also delicious as a topping for bubbling hot cheese on toast.

Oven method: Put the quartered capsicums skin side down onto a lightly oiled cake tin. Bake in a preheated oven at 220°C (425°F) for 15–20 minutes, or until the capsicums are soft and their skins start to blacken. Remove from the oven and allow to cool for a minute or so. Either steam in a plastic bag or plunge them into cold water to remove the skins.

Moroccan Carrots

Serves 4–6

Thanks to Sydney foodie Frances Abdallaoui for this great carrot salad, previously published in *Australian House & Garden* magazine in a collection of my favourite recipes.

---

750 g large carrots
1 clove garlic, peeled and crushed
½ level teaspoon paprika
½ level teaspoon ground cumin
½ level teaspoon chopped fresh chilli
2 tablespoons fresh lemon juice
2 tablespoons olive oil
pinch sugar
salt and freshly ground black pepper, to taste
3 or 4 sprigs fresh coriander leaves
6 fresh dates, finely sliced

Peel the carrots, then cut into thick slices or chunks. Cook in boiling, salted water until 'just' tender, then drain. Meanwhile, in a screwtop jar, combine the garlic, paprika, cumin and chilli, then add the lemon juice, olive oil, sugar, salt and pepper. Shake well to combine. Pour over the drained carrots while they're still warm. Scatter over the coriander leaves and the dates and serve warm as an accompaniment to a grill or barbecue (especially good with lamb or fish).

Glazed Tarragon Carrots

Serves 6

The tarragon and buttery caramel glaze add another dimension to carrots.

500 g carrots, peeled and cut into julienne (matchstick lengths)
pinch of salt
1 heaped tablespoon butter
1 level teaspoon brown sugar
2 good pinches of dried tarragon

Put the carrots in a saucepan and barely cover with water. Add the salt and simmer for about 10 minutes, then drain. Melt the butter in a saucepan, then add the drained carrots, brown sugar and tarragon. Toss over a gentle heat until glazed (the carrots burn easily, so don't walk away and leave them). Serve hot as a vegetable accompaniment.

CARROT AND POTATO FRITTERS

Makes 10–12

250 g carrots (3 medium)
1 medium potato
1 small onion
2 eggs
2 level tablespoons self-raising flour
salt and freshly ground black pepper, to taste
1 tablespoon chopped parsley or coriander
oil, for frying

Peel the carrots, potato and onion. Grate on the coarse blade of a grater into a bowl (see Note). Add the eggs, flour, salt, pepper and parsley, and mix well. Heat sufficient oil in a frying pan to shallow-fry the fritters. Drop level tablespoons of the mixture into the hot oil and fry for a few minutes or until golden, turning once. Remove to crumpled paper towels to drain. Serve hot as a snack or light lunch.
Note: Grated potato discolours quickly, so prepare it just before cooking.

CAULIFLOWER CHEESE

Serves 6

1 small cauliflower, trimmed and cut into florets
salt
50 g butter
4 level tablespoons plain flour
3 cups milk
1 heaped teaspoon mixed mustard (French or German-style)
tiny pinch of cayenne pepper
1 cup coarsely grated mature cheddar cheese
1 tablespoon finely grated Parmesan cheese
1 cup buttered crumbs (see below)

Preheat the oven to 200°–230°C (400°–450°F). Cut a slit in the stems of each of the cauliflower florets, so that they cook evenly. Put the cauliflower in a saucepan and cover with cold water. Add a pinch of salt and bring to the boil. Cover loosely with a lid and cook for about 5 minutes (the cauliflower should be crispy tender — the flavour is too strong when it is overcooked).

Meanwhile, melt the butter in a saucepan, then stir in the flour with a wooden spoon to make a roux. Turn the heat down and let the roux cook, *without browning*, for 1 minute. Remove from the heat and gradually stir in the milk. Return to the heat and stir constantly until the sauce boils and thickens. Give it a good beat with the wooden spoon to make it smooth and shiny. Add the mustard and season with good pinch salt and the cayenne pepper.

Arrange the cooked cauliflower in a shallow ovenproof dish, then pour over the mustard sauce. Sprinkle over the the cheddar cheese and the Parmesan, then finish with the buttered crumbs. Bake in the oven for 15–20 minutes. Serve hot.

Buttered Crumbs: Make 1 cup fresh breadcrumbs in a food processor using 3 to 4 slices stale white bread, then add 15 g softened butter and process briefly.

Mini Corn Flapjacks

Serves 4–6

These little corn pancakes have a light, crisp crust and are creamy in the middle.

1 x 440 g can corn kernels
2 young spring onions
¼ cup self-raising flour
½ cup plain flour (white or wholemeal)
good pinch of salt
1 heaped teaspoon brown sugar
1 egg
⅔ cup milk
freshly ground black pepper, to taste
olive oil, for cooking

Empty the can of corn into a strainer and set aside to drain. Trim the spring onions, then slice or chop finely, using the white portion and including just a little of the green.

To make the pancake batter, put the self-raising flour, plain flour, salt, sugar, egg and spring onions into a food processor bowl or a mixing bowl. Add the milk and beat until well mixed. Add the corn kernels, then season with pepper to taste.

Heat a thin layer of olive oil in a frying pan, then cook the flapjacks in batches (don't crowd the pan). Allow one tablespoon of the mixture for each one, and leave plenty of room between for turning. Keep the heat low so they cook in the middle, allowing about 2 minutes on each side. These flapjacks are best when served hot from the pan and are good for breakfast, brunch or lunch. Bacon makes a delicious accompaniment.

Sam's Baked Eggplant

Serves 4

I learned about this Italian way of cooking eggplant when my assistant, Margaret Ientile, cooked these for our lunch. Margaret's dad is Italian and this is one of his specialities.

2 x 350 g purple eggplants (they should be fresh and firm)
2 large cloves garlic
3 cups soft fresh breadcrumbs
2 cups freshly grated Parmesan cheese
⅓ cup chopped fresh parsley
½ level teaspoon salt
freshly ground black pepper, to taste
extra virgin olive oil

Preheat the oven to 200ºC (400ºF). Cut the eggplants in halves lengthwise, sprinkle with water and microwave in two batches (covered loosely with plastic wrap), allowing 4 minutes on high for each batch. (Alternatively, if you don't own a microwave, parboil the eggplants in water for 4 minutes). Scoop out the flesh, leaving a 1 cm wall on the sides. Reserve both flesh and shells.

In a food processor, chop the garlic, then add the breadcrumbs, eggplant flesh, Parmesan cheese, parsley, salt and pepper to taste. Process until smooth.

Divide the mixture into four portions and return to the eggplant shells. Place on a foil-lined baking tray and drizzle generously with olive oil. Bake in the oven for 30–40 minutes, until slightly puffy and light golden brown. Serve immediately, straight from the oven.

Caponata

Serves 4–6

This Italian sweet and sour eggplant salad makes a delicious accompaniment to char-grilled or poached fish.

---

1 large firm eggplant (about 500 g)
2 level teaspoons salt
4 tablespoons olive oil
1 stick celery, diced
1 level tablespoon capers
50 g small green olives
1 onion, peeled and thinly sliced
500 g ripe tomatoes, peeled and chopped
½ cup (125 mL) water
2 teaspoons sugar
2 tablespoon white wine vinegar
1 teaspoon balsamic vinegar
salt and freshly ground black pepper, to taste
2 tablespoons pine nuts, toasted

Cut the eggplant into large cubes (leaving the skin on), then put the cubes into a colander, sprinkle with salt and leave for 30 minutes. When the time has elapsed, press down on the eggplant cubes to remove any excess moisture and rinse under cold running water. Pat dry with a clean cloth.

Heat 3 tablespoons of the oil in a large frying pan over a low heat and fry the eggplant until golden (don't crowd the pan, cook in two batches if necessary). Remove from the heat and drain the eggplant on paper towels.

Blanch the celery, capers and olives in boiling water. Drain immediately.

To make the sauce, heat the remaining olive oil in a frying pan and cook the onion slowly for 5–10 minutes. Add the tomatoes and cook for about 15 minutes, adding ½ cup of water to create some juice. Add the sugar, wine vinegar and the blanched celery, capers and olives, then stir in the cooked eggplant. Add the balsamic vinegar, then the salt and pepper to taste. Serve 'just warm' or at room temperature sprinkled with pine nuts to go with char-grilled or poached fish.

Couscous

Serves 4

Couscous is a durum wheat semolina which is traditionally hand-rolled then steamed in a 'couscoussier' (a special couscous cooker) over a simmering stew. A modern version of this traditional idea is the pre-cooked instant couscous, which is mostly imported from France and available in colourful packets at gourmet food shops and delicatessens. This 'instant' couscous takes only 5 minutes to prepare: simply follow the instructions on the packet and serve. However, if you have the time, additional steaming of the instant couscous will produce a lighter and fluffier grain. A saucepan, colander and tea towel make a very satisfactory improvised 'couscoussier'.

250 g (1¼ cups) instant couscous
1 cup (250 mL) boiling water
2 tablespoons melted butter or olive oil
salt, to taste

Put the couscous into a shallow dish, pour over the boiling water and let stand for a few minutes until the couscous swells and absorbs all the water; transfer to a colander.

Place the colander over a saucepan of boiling water (the level of the water should be below the couscous and the colander should fit the saucepan snugly). Fold a damp tea towel diagonally and tie it around the seam where the colander and saucepan meet (so steam will be forced through the couscous). Steam the couscous, uncovered, for about 10 minutes, and then add the butter and salt to taste. Fork through the couscous lightly and continue to steam for a further 5 minutes.

Couscous is a good accompaniment to a casserole or stew, but if you wish to serve it with another dish, always serve couscous with plenty of sauce or gravy.

Mushrooms on Toast

Serves 4

The large dark mushroom flats have the most flavour.

---

60 g butter
1 bunch young spring onions, trimmed and chopped (white part only)
400 g large, dark mushroom flats, sliced (if not available, use mushroom cups)
2 level tablespoons plain flour
2 cups (500 mL) milk
salt and freshly ground black pepper, to taste
tiny pinch cayenne pepper (optional)
1 bunch of fresh chives, chopped
thick slices of hot, buttered toast

Heat the butter in a large frying pan until melted. Add the spring onions and mushrooms, and toss quickly over a high heat to coat with the butter. Cover and cook for a few minutes more to soften the mushrooms (this saves using too much butter). Remove the lid, sprinkle over the flour and stir through. Add the milk and stir constantly until the sauce boils and thickens. Turn off the heat and make the toast. Reheat the mushrooms, season to taste with salt, pepper, and the cayenne (if using). Thin with more milk if necessary, then add the chives and spoon the mushroom mixture over the hot, buttered toast. Serve immediately.

Mushroom Sauce for Steak: Thin the sauce with an additional ½ cup milk, then spoon over freshly grilled, pan-fried or barbecued rump or Scotch fillet steak.

Soft Polenta with Mushrooms and Tomatoes

Serves 4

Make the sauce first so the polenta can be served as soon as it's ready. I included this dish in a menu once to cater for a vegetarian guest, and the meat-eaters all tucked into it and asked for the recipe!

1 onion, peeled and sliced
2 tablespoons olive oil
400 g mushrooms, sliced
3 large ripe tomatoes, chopped or grated (or use 2 cups Italian-style tomato cooking sauce)
10 fresh basil leaves
salt and freshly ground black pepper, to taste

Soft Polenta
4 cups (1 litre) water
1 level teaspoon salt
1 cup coarse polenta (see Note)
1 tablespoon softened butter
2 tablespoons freshly grated Parmesan cheese

extra fresh basil, sliced, for serving
extra freshly grated Parmesan cheese, for serving

Put the onion and 1 tablespoon of the oil into a large frying pan. Cook over a low heat for 5 minutes or so, stirring often, until the onion is soft and glossy. Add the remaining 1 tablespoon of oil to the pan, then add half the mushrooms. Let the mushrooms soften, then push to one side of the pan and sauté the remainder. Add the tomatoes and a few tablespoons of water (or the Italian-style tomato cooking sauce). Cover and simmer for about 10 minutes. Turn off the heat and set the tomato mixture aside while preparing the polenta. Just before serving, reheat the sauce and season with salt and pepper to taste, and the extra basil leaves. Serve warm over the freshly cooked polenta.

Soft Polenta

To make the polenta, bring the water and salt to the boil in a large, wide-based saucepan. Measure out the polenta onto a plate or sheet of baking paper. The polenta should be added very gradually, a handful at a time. Allow it to trickle through your closed fist into the rapidly boiling water while you whisk furiously with the other hand (use a sturdy whisk or wooden spoon to stir). Reduce the heat as the polenta thickens to prevent spitting. Stir until it starts to leave the sides of the pan, then cover with a lid and turn the heat as low as possible. Cook for a further 20 minutes, stirring often. Add some extra water gradually to make it light and soft, depending on how long it cooks. Stir in the butter and Parmesan cheese, then taste and add extra salt if necessary. Divide the polenta between 4 heated plates, dig a little hole in the centre of each one then pour in hot mushroom and tomato sauce. Serve immediately scattered with fresh sliced basil and extra Parmesan. Serve immediately while the polenta is smooth and creamy.

Note: Polenta develops a skin if left to stand, so that's why it's best to serve right away.

Quick-cooking Polenta: If using a pre-cooked quick polenta, simply follow the instructions on the packet — it takes only 3 minutes to cook but it is not as silky as the real thing.

Mashed Potato

Serves 4–5

750 g potatoes, peeled and cut into large chunks (see hints on choosing the right potato)
pinch of salt
1–2 heaped teaspoons soft butter
½ cup hot milk
salt and freshly ground black pepper, to taste
pinch of nutmeg
chopped chives or parsley, to garnish

Put the potatoes in a saucepan and barely cover with water. Add a pinch of salt, then cover the pan with a lid. Bring to boil, then reduce the heat and simmer for 20–25 minutes (make sure they're cooked thoroughly, undercooking often causes lumpy potatoes). Drain, leaving about 1 tablespoon of the hot potato water in the pan, then mash with a potato masher or fork, and add the butter and hot milk. Beat with a wooden spoon or wire whisk (don't put in a food processor as this makes the potatoes gluey). Season to taste with salt and pepper, and add the nutmeg. Thin slightly with extra milk if necessary. To keep hot for a short time after mashing, cover tightly and use a heat diffuser under the saucepan. If holding for 10 minutes or so, pour a little extra hot milk over the top, then stir this through the potatoes before serving.

Champ or Irish Mashed Potato: Cook 4 sliced spring onions in 1 tablespoon butter for a few minutes without browning. Stir the buttery shallots through the mashed potatoes before adding the hot milk. Mix gently; don't beat too much.

Sour Cream Mashed Potato: Drain the potatoes, leaving 3–4 tablespoons of the potato water in the saucepan (this hot water makes the potatoes extra light). Mash the potatoes in the saucepan, then add 1 heaped tablespoon sour cream and beat with a wire whisk until the potatoes are light and fluffy. Lighten with extra boiling water. Serve topped with chopped chives and season.

The Right Potato

Fluffy mashed potato: Use mealy potatoes such as Pontiac, Sebago, Toolangi Delight, Nicola, Spunta or King Edward.

Creamy Potato Puree: Use Desirée or Bintje for a creamy mashed potato with lots of flavour.

POTATO AND CELERIAC MASH

Serves 5–6

Cooking the potatoes with celeriac gives them a creamy texture and a mild celery flavour.

---

600 g potatoes
300–350 g (1 medium-sized) celeriac
good pinch of salt
1 heaped tablespoon sour cream or 30 g soft butter
4–6 tablespoons hot milk
salt and freshly ground black pepper, to taste

Peel the potatoes and celeriac, then cut into chunks. Put in a saucepan and barely cover with water. Add the salt, cover the pan and simmer until the vegetables are tender, about 25 minutes. Drain off the water leaving about 1 tablespoon water in the pan, then mash the vegetables well. Add the sour cream and sufficient hot milk to make a light and fluffy mash. Season to taste with salt and pepper. Serve hot as an accompaniment. This dish is good with grilled steak, roast beef, lamb chops or lamb stew.

OLIVE OIL MASH

Serves 6

Olive oil is used instead of butter to enrich this potato and garlic mash. Serve as an accompaniment to crunchy fried fish in batter.

1 kg potatoes, peeled and cut into large chunks
2–3 large cloves garlic, peeled
good pinch of salt
2 tablespoons extra virgin olive oil
salt and freshly ground black pepper, to taste
chopped fresh parsley, to garnish

Put the potatoes in a saucepan with the garlic. Barely cover with water, add salt, cover tightly with a lid and simmer for 20–25 minutes (undercooking often causes lumpy potatoes). Drain the potatoes and garlic, reserving a good ½ cup of the cooking water. Mash the potatoes and garlic well, then add the olive oil and reserved cooking water. Season well with salt and pepper, and beat until light and fluffy using a wooden spoon or wire whisk. Add extra hot water if necessary to keep the potatoes moist and light. Serve hot sprinkled with the parsley.

POTATO GRATIN

Serves 6

This is a great potato gratin recipe, but don't make the mistake of soaking the potatoes in water prior to cooking as this removes the starch essential for the creamy texture.

---

1 kg potatoes (Desirée are good)
1¾ cups (440 mL) milk
¼ cup (65 mL) cream
1 large clove garlic, peeled and crushed
½ level teaspoon salt, to taste
tiny pinch of ground nutmeg
freshly ground black pepper, to taste
2 tablespoons melted butter
2 level tablespoons freshly grated Parmesan cheese

Preheat the oven to 200°C (400°F). Peel the potatoes and cut into 3 mm slices ($2 coin thickness). Put in a large saucepan with the milk, cream and garlic. Bring to the boil, then reduce the heat and simmer for 5 minutes only, stirring often to prevent the milk catching on the bottom of the saucepan. Season with salt, nutmeg and a generous quantity of pepper. Transfer into a well-greased, shallow ovenproof dish and spread out evenly.

Brush the top layer of potatoes with the butter, then sprinkle evenly with the Parmesan. Bake in the oven for about 1 hour, or until the potatoes are tender and creamy, and the top is golden brown. Potato Gratin is a good potato dish for casual entertaining. Serve with a plain roast chicken, roast beef or grilled veal chops.

Farmer's Potato Bake

Serves 6

Geoff and Bronwyn Dobson, in Victoria's Goulburn Valley, grow a variety of 'gourmet' potatoes to supply many of the top restaurants. When I requested their favourite recipe, they didn't hesitate and immediately nominated this delicious herbed potato bake with onions and balsamic vinegar.

1 kg Desirée potatoes
2 medium onions
2 tablespoons olive oil
2 tablespoons balsamic vinegar
1 level teaspoon dried thyme or use 4 large sprigs of fresh sage
½ level teaspoon salt
freshly ground black pepper, to taste
chopped fresh parsley or basil, to garnish

Preheat the oven to 220°C (425°F). Wash the potatoes (they can be peeled or cooked with the skin on), then cut into 3 cm chunks. Peel the onions, then cut lengthwise into eighths. Put the oil into a large, shallow baking dish. Add the potatoes and onions, then cover tightly with foil. Bake in the oven for about 45 minutes.

Remove the baking dish of potatoes and onions from the oven, take off the foil and sprinkle the balsamic vinegar evenly over the potatoes. Scatter with the thyme. Season with the salt and a generous quantity of black pepper. Increase the oven temperature to very hot (230°C/450°F) and cook uncovered for a further 30–40 minutes, or until the potatoes are tender and slightly crisp and golden on the edges. Sprinkle with the parsley or basil. Serve hot as an accompaniment.

Coriander Potatoes in Fresh Tomato Sauce

Serves 4

Serve these spiced potatoes as an accompaniment to fish, meat or poultry, or serve as part of a vegetarian meal.

---

4 medium potatoes (about 600 g)
1 small onion, peeled and finely chopped
1 tablespoon light vegetable oil
1 level teaspoon ground coriander
1 level teaspoon ground cumin
1 chilli, seeded and finely chopped, or a good pinch of chilli flakes
2 large ripe tomatoes, chopped or grated (see hint following)
½ cup water
good pinch of salt
¼ cup fresh coriander leaves (about ½ bunch)

Peel the potatoes and cut into large cubes (about 2 cm). Parboil in salted water for 5 minutes (don't overcook as they need to hold their shape), then drain. Put the onion into a wok with the oil, then stir-fry over a gentle heat until the onion is soft. Add the well-drained potato cubes, toss around to coat with the oil and sprinkle with the ground coriander, cumin and chilli. Turn the heat up to high and stir-fry the potatoes with the onion and spices until the potatoes are slightly crisp.

Add the tomatoes, water and salt. Bring to the boil, then cover with a saucepan lid and reduce the heat. Let the potatoes cook gently in the spicy tomato broth for about 10 minutes, adding an extra tablespoon of water only as necessary to keep the sauce moist. Add half the fresh coriander leaves to the sauce and cook for a minute longer. Serve sprinkled with the remaining coriander leaves.

Grated tomatoes: To obtain an instant fresh tomato puree, cut tomatoes into halves, then grate the cut side on the large holes of a grater, flattening your hand as you go. When finished, only the skin of the tomato will be left.

Creamy Potato Salad

Serves 6

This salad is especially good when served with a sizzling hot Wiener schnitzel or crumbed veal cutlet.

750 g small new potatoes (or use a waxy potato such as Desirée, Petrone or Nicola)
good pinch of salt
2–3 sprigs of mint
squeeze of lemon
1 level tablespoon white salad onion, very finely chopped
4 spring onions (white part only), chopped
1 tablespoon vinaigrette dressing (2 parts oil, 1 part vinegar or lemon juice, and a little crushed garlic)
½ cup egg mayonnaise
juice of ¼ lemon
salt and freshly ground black pepper, to taste
1 tablespoon capers
1 tablespoon finely chopped parsley
4–6 sprigs of mint, chopped

Peel the potatoes and put them into a saucepan. Add enough water to barely cover the potatoes, then add a good pinch salt and a couple of mint sprigs. If using white new potatoes, add a squeeze of lemon juice. Simmer (loosely covered) until the potatoes are just tender, about 12–15 minutes, then drain immediately so they don't overcook and break up. When cool, cut into thick slices and put into a bowl with the onion, spring onion and vinaigrette dressing and toss together. Fold through the mayonnaise, then add a good squeeze of lemon juice and the salt, pepper, capers and parsley. Just before serving add the mint (mint discolours on standing, so always chop and add to a salad at the last minute). Serve the salad cold and refrigerate any leftovers.

Note: Adding the lemon juice to the potatoes will prevent them turning black during or after cooking. When potatoes blacken it is not harmful but just an indication that they contain a high level of iron. Lemon juice or a dash of vinegar added to the cooking water usually overcomes this problem.

Favourite Green Salad

Serves 4–6

1 large cos lettuce
1 mignonette lettuce
1 butter or oakleaf lettuce
1 celery heart (tender inside part), chopped
1 firm, ripe avocado
2 firm vine-ripened tomatoes, diced
Mustard Lime Dressing (see following)
4 tablespoons freshly grated Parmesan cheese
fresh herbs (such as basil or chives)

Wash the lettuce, separate into leaves, then drain in a colander. Store in a crisper until ready to serve. Arrange the large outside cos lettuce leaves in a big salad bowl (these are just for presentation). Fill the centre with mixed salad leaves and the celery heart. Cut the avocado into thick slices and add to the salad with the tomatoes. Drizzle the Mustard Lime Dressing over the salad, then scatter the Parmesan cheese over the top. Scatter over some torn basil leaves or sprinkle with chopped chives. Serve immediately.

Mustard Lime Dressing

1 teaspoon mixed French or German-style mustard
1 clove garlic, crushed
1½ tablespoons fresh lime juice
3 tablespoons extra virgin olive oil (or use half light vegetable oil)
freshly ground black pepper, to taste

Mix the mustard and crushed garlic in a small jug or bowl. Gradually add the lime juice, then whisk in the olive oil. Add a little more olive oil if you like. Season with pepper to taste. Stir well or shake in a small jar before serving. Store in the refrigerator and use within a few days.

Turkish Pilaf Rice

Serves 8

This moist and tender rice is flavoured with chicken stock and onions, and studded with pine nuts and currants. It works well as an accompaniment to a lamb roast or with barbecued lamb kebabs.

---

2 cups long-grain rice
2½ level teaspoons salt (sounds a lot but it is rinsed off)
4 cups (1 litre) boiling water
40 g butter
1 onion, peeled and chopped
¼ cup pine nuts
3 cups (750 mL) chicken stock
2 tablespoons currants
1 level teaspoon sugar
freshly ground black pepper, to taste
½ cup chopped fresh dill

Put the rice into a mixing bowl with 2 teaspoons of the salt, then pour over the boiling water. Stir well, then allow to stand for 20 minutes. Drain into a sieve and wash well under cold, running water.

Meanwhile, melt the butter in large saucepan. Add the onion, then reduce the heat and cook the onion gently for a good 5 minutes to develop the flavour before adding the pine nuts. Continue to cook, stirring occasionally, until the pine nuts are just starting to turn golden. Add the drained rice; stir well and cook a further 5 minutes over a low heat so the rice is well coated with the butter.

Pour in the chicken stock and add the currants, sugar and the remaining ½ level teaspoon of salt, plus a generous quantity of pepper. Increase the heat and bring to the boil, then cook over a medium heat for 15 minutes. Turn the heat to very low, cover and cook for a further 5–10 minutes until the rice has absorbed all the stock. Add the dill (the dill should be added just before serving to preserve the colour and flavour) and serve hot.

Note: If making ahead of time, refrigerate the pilaf, then reheat uncovered over a low heat or in the microwave.

Creamy Potato Salad (page 94) and Crumbed Veal

Favourite Green Salad (page 95)

Baked Ricotta with Gremolata (page 111)

Eggs Benedict (page 112)

Panna Cotta (page 124)

Steamed Marmalade Pudding (page 128) and Lemon Delicious (page 120)

Melting Moments (page 143) and My Favourite Gingerbread Biscuits (page 140)

Almond Friands (page 144) and Lemon Sauce Cake (page 148)

Shepherd's Salad

Serves 4–6

This refreshing Turkish salad is good to serve as an accompaniment to a barbecue or grill.

1 medium Spanish onion, peeled and very finely sliced
salt, to prepare onion
6 firmly ripe egg tomatoes or 3 medium tomatoes, diced
2 small Lebanese cucumbers, diced
6 small round radishes, thinly sliced
½ cup chopped fresh parsley
2 tablespoons fresh lemon juice
1 tablespoon extra virgin olive oil
salt and freshly ground black pepper, to taste

Put the onion slices onto a plate. Sprinkle with a little salt. Leave for a few minutes, then rub the salt in with your fingertips. Rinse the onion in a sieve under cold running water. Pat dry and put into a salad bowl. Add the tomatoes, cucumbers, radishes and parsley and mix together. Just before serving make a dressing with the lemon juice, olive oil and salt and pepper to taste. Whisk well together then pour over the salad. Toss until the vegetables glisten, then serve.

TOMATO AND BASIL SALAD

Serves 6

This salad looks gorgeous and tastes good too.

---

6 firm, vine-ripened tomatoes, sliced
½ bunch fresh basil
1 celery heart (tender inside part), finely diced
1 punnet cherry tomatoes, cut in halves
1 tablespoon extra virgin olive oil
2 teaspoons fresh lemon or lime juice
2 teaspoons balsamic vinegar
freshly ground black pepper and rock salt, to taste

Overlap the sliced tomatoes on a large flat platter, then tuck a basil leaf in between each slice. Scatter over the celery, then pile the cherry tomatoes in the middle. Sprinkle the salad with oil, lemon juice and balsamic vinegar, then season with black pepper and, at the very last minute, with a little salt. Garnish in the middle with a sprig of basil. Serve immediately.

Tomato and Bocconcini Salad: Slice 6 bocconcini (fresh mozzarella) thinly. On a platter, overlap alternating slices of tomato and bocconcini and whole basil leaves. Scatter over the celery, then dress the salad as described above.

SNACKS

Teriyaki Chicken

Kedgeree

Veal and Ham Brawn

Macaroni Cheese

Easy No-yeast Pizza

Vietnamese Fresh Spring Rolls

Hummus bi Tahini

David's Easy Hummus

Guacamole

Baked Ricotta with Gremolata

Eggs Benedict

Fluffy Scrambled Eggs

Teriyaki Chicken

Serves 8

A popular finger food at parties when you want to serve something more substantial than dips 'n chips.

2 kg small chicken legs, or chicken wings
1 cup salt-reduced Japanese soy sauce
2 level tablespoons honey
2 large cloves garlic, crushed
5 cm chunk fresh ginger, peeled and sliced
1 cup (250 mL) water
2 tablespoons sesame seeds

If using chicken wings, remove and discard wingtips. Put the soy sauce into a large dish, add the honey (warmed slightly if necessary so that it mixes easily), garlic and ginger. Add the chicken legs or wings, and mix well. Cover and marinate in the refrigerator for an hour, or overnight.

When ready to cook, preheat the oven to 180°C (350°F). Pour off the marinade into a large saucepan and add the water. Add half the chicken and simmer gently for about 15 minutes (don't overcook or chicken legs will fall apart). Transfer the chicken to a baking dish, reserving the broth in the saucepan. Cook the remaining chicken in the reserved broth, then add to the baking dish. Moisten the chicken with a couple of tablespoons of the broth and bake in the oven for about 10 minutes, or until the chicken has turned the most beautiful golden colour.

Meanwhile, shake or stir the sesame seeds in a dry pan or wok over a low heat until they turn golden (watch them carefully as they burn easily). Place the hot chicken on a big platter, sprinkle over the toasted sesame seeds and garnish with bright green herbs or citrus leaves. Serve immediately as a finger food with drinks.

Note: To give you an idea of quantities, there are about 10 chicken legs and 12 chicken wings per kg.

KEDGEREE

Serves 6

Here's a recipe that you don't see much these days, but it is such a wonderful dish that combines good things most people like to eat. Perhaps it is time for a revival.

3/4 cup uncooked long-grain rice
500 g smoked cod or smoked haddock
3 hard-boiled eggs, peeled and chopped
2 level teaspoons mild curry powder
1/4 cup fresh lemon juice
4 spring onions
2 level tablespoons chopped fresh parsley
pinch of ground nutmeg
tiny pinch of cayenne pepper
4 tablespoons cream
60 g butter, cut into cubes
extra chopped parsley and lemon wedges, for serving

Preheat the oven to 180°C (350°F). Cook the rice in rapidly boiling water for 10–12 minutes, or until cooked but still in firm, separate grains (please don't over-cook). Drain the rice into a colander and rinse under cold, running water. Set aside.

    Put the smoked cod into a frying pan or saucepan, and cover with fresh cold water. Bring to the boil, then pour off this water and replace with fresh cold water. Simmer until the fish is tender, about 10 minutes, then allow to cool. Break the fish into large flakes, removing any skin. Put the cooked rice, flaked fish and hard-boiled eggs into a large bowl. Sprinkle over the curry powder and mix through evenly, then mix in the lemon juice. Trim the spring onions and slice very thinly, including a little of the green stems, then add to the rice mixture with the parsley, nutmeg and cayenne pepper. Moisten with the cream and mix together lightly, using two forks. Transfer to a shallow, ovenproof dish, toss with the forks again to keep it light, then dot with the butter and bake in the oven until heated through, about 15–20 minutes. Garnish with parsley and lemon wedges. Serve with triangles of thin unbuttered toast.

Veal and Ham Brawn

Good homemade brawn is a marvellous thing, although you don't often see it these days.

2 veal shanks, sawn
1 brown onion, peeled and halved
¼ cup (65 mL) white wine
1 stick celery, roughly chopped
1 carrot, roughly chopped
12 cups (3 litres) water
1 bay leaf
1 teaspoon black peppercorns
1 teaspoon dried tarragon
few sprigs of fresh parsley
2 ham hocks
1 level teaspoon gelatine dissolved in 1 tablespoon boiling water
1 teaspoon Worcestershire sauce
½ teaspoon mustard powder
good pinch of ground nutmeg
1 tablespoon fresh lemon juice or white vinegar
4 hard-boiled eggs, sliced
extra fresh parsley, chopped
freshly ground black pepper

Preheat the oven to 200°C (400°F). Put the veal shanks into a greased baking dish with the onion and bake in the oven for 30 minutes. Add the wine, celery and carrot, and bake for a further 15 minutes (roasting the meat and vegetables produces a better flavour in the stock). Transfer the contents of the baking dish to a big saucepan or boiler and add the water, bay leaf, peppercorns, tarragon and a few sprigs of parsley. *Do not add any salt.* Cover and simmer slowly for about 2 hours, skimming from time to time.

Meanwhile, simmer the ham hocks in water to remove any excess salt, then add to the stock during the last hour of cooking. Strain the stock into a container and refrigerate. Discard the bones from the meats, cut the chunky pieces of ham into smallish cubes and set aside. Put the tender veal onto a board and shred with two forks, then chop well. Add to the ham.

Skim the stock and measure 2 cups into a saucepan. Boil to reduce slightly (omit this step if the stock tastes salty), then add the dissolved gelatine. Flavour with the Worcestershire sauce, mustard, nutmeg and lemon juice. Pour a thin layer of this liquid into the base of two small basins or six individual cups (reserving the remaining flavoured stock). Refrigerate until set, then arrange the egg and extra parsley on top of the jellied stock. Add some more chopped parsley and lots of pepper to the meat, then stack the meat into the moulds. Pour in just enough of the reserved flavoured stock to cover the meat. Cover each one, then weigh down and stand in the refrigerator until set. Store in the refrigerator until ready to use. Turn out, then serve with a salad or in sandwiches. This brawn is especially good served on hot, buttered toast.

Leftover stock: Freeze the remainder of the rich veal stock to add flavour to casseroles, soups and sauces.

Macaroni Cheese

Serves 4

⅔ cup (100 g) macaroni
2 level tablespoons butter
2 level tablespoons flour
2½ cups (625 mL) milk
100 g Gruyère cheese, grated (or use a tasty matured cheddar or mozzarella)
60 g pecorino or Parmesan cheese, finely grated
½ teaspoon salt
1 level teaspoon mustard powder
pinch of cayenne pepper
4 rashers bacon, trimmed and chopped
1 cup soft breadcrumbs tossed in 1 level tablespoon melted butter

Preheat the oven to 230°C (450°F). Cook the macaroni in boiling, salted water for 20 minutes, then drain. Melt the butter in a saucepan, then add the flour and stir with a wooden spoon over a low heat, without browning, for a minute or so. Remove from the heat, gradually stir in the milk, then return to a medium heat and stir until the sauce boils and thickens (the sauce may seem a little thin, but don't worry — it will thicken up when cheese is added). Add the Gruyère cheese, mix through then add the pecorino. Season with the salt, mustard and cayenne, then add the drained macaroni. Cook the bacon in a small pan until lightly cooked (or cook in the microwave between two paper towels, allowing 2 minutes on full power). Add the bacon to the macaroni cheese mixture, then transfer into a suitable ovenproof dish (or use individual ramekins or small soufflé dishes). Cover with the buttered crumbs, then bake in the oven for about 10–15 minutes, until the sauce is bubbling hot and the crumbs are crunchy and golden brown. Serve hot with a side salad of mixed lettuce and ripe tomatoes.

Easy No-Yeast Pizza

Serves 6–8

A handy recipe to whip up with the ingredients from the cupboard.

1 cup plain flour
1 cup self-raising flour
good pinch of cayenne pepper or ½ teaspoon paprika
75 g butter
⅔ cup milk or water
2 large onions, peeled and sliced
2 tablespoons olive oil
1½ cups grated mature cheddar cheese
2 large firmly ripe tomatoes, thinly sliced
1 level teaspoon dried oregano
2 eggs
250 g chopped bacon pieces

Preheat the oven to 220°C (425°F). Sift the plain flour, self-raising flour and salt into a mixing bowl. Add the cayenne and rub in the butter. Make into a scone dough with the milk, then turn out onto a floured surface. Knead with a little extra flour. Roll out thinly using a lightly floured rolling pin to fit an oiled pizza plate (32–36 cm) or Swiss roll tin.

Put the onions into a frying pan with the oil and cook over a low heat for about 10 minutes, until the onions are soft and glossy (this develops the flavour). Spread the onions and any cooking oil from the pan over the pizza dough, then sprinkle with a layer of grated cheese. Cover with a layer of tomato, then more cheese and the oregano. Beat the eggs, then pour evenly over the mixture (this helps to set the topping and makes it easier to cut). Scatter over the chopped bacon, then bake the pizza in the oven for about 45 minutes. Cut into wedges and serve hot with salad.

Vietnamese Fresh Spring Rolls

Serves 6

500 g cooked medium prawns, peeled and deveined
50 g fine rice vermicelli
2 teaspoons fresh lime or lemon juice
1 teaspoon fish sauce (nam pla)
pinch of sugar
125 g Chinese barbecued pork, thinly sliced
1 x 375 g packet rice paper squares (available at Asian grocers)
1 butter lettuce, washed and separated into leaves
small bunch of fresh mint
few sprigs of fresh coriander (optional)
1 small carrot, coarsely grated

Place the prawns in a dish, cover and refrigerate until ready to make the rolls. Put the rice vermicelli into a bowl, then pour over enough boiling water to cover. Leave to soak for 2 minutes, then drain well and transfer to a cutting board. Slice into short lengths (this makes the rolls easier to eat), then put into a bowl. Mix the lime juice, fish sauce and sugar together in a small bowl, then add to the noodles and toss well.

When ready to make the rolls, assemble the pork, prawns, vermicelli, lettuce, mint and coriander (if using) and carrot. Pour some boiling water into a wide, shallow dish. Dip the rice paper into hot water and, as soon as it softens, remove to a flat serving plate. Place a small piece of lettuce on one end of the paper, then top with a few thin slices of pork. Add a little pile of noodles, some carrot and a couple of mint leaves. Roll up halfway, tucking in the sides of the papers. Add 2 prawns (or 3 if they're small), then finish rolling. Turn the roll over so the seam is underneath. Repeat this process until all the rice papers are used.

Serve with small bowls of dipping sauces such as Nuoc Cham or Chilli Plum Sauce (see below). The rolls are best served immediately, but if making an hour or so before serving, cover them lightly with plastic wrap or a dampened, well wrung-out teatowel to keep the rice paper soft, then refrigerate until ready to serve.

Hint: If only large prawns are available, halve lengthwise so they're easy to roll.

Nuoc Cham

Makes 1 cup

1/4 cup white vinegar
1/4 cup sugar
1/2 cup (125 mL) water
1/4 cup fish sauce (nam pla)
3 cloves garlic, crushed
2 chillies, seeded and finely chopped
2 teaspoons fresh lime or lemon juice
1/2 small carrot, coarsely grated

Put the vinegar, sugar and water into a small saucepan and simmer for a few minutes, until the sugar dissolves. Remove from the heat, add the fish sauce, garlic, chillies and fresh lime juice. Allow to cool, then store in refrigerator. To serve, put the sauce into a small dish and add the carrot.

Chilli Plum Sauce

Makes about 2/3 cup

4 tablespoons plum sauce
2 tablespoons light soy sauce
1 tablespoon tomato sauce
sweet chilli sauce, to taste
few drops of sesame oil
squeeze of lemon or lime juice (optional)

Mix the plum sauce, soy sauce and tomato sauce together, then add the chilli sauce and sesame oil to taste. Add a squeeze of lemon or lime juice if you like to balance the sweetness.

Hummus bi Tahini

Serves 8–10

Serve as a dip with triangles of Lebanese bread or as a dressing with barbecued lamb kebabs.

2/3 cup (125 g) dried chickpeas, soaked in cold water overnight
4 large cloves garlic, peeled and crushed
1/2 cup (125 mL) freshly squeezed lemon juice (usually 3 lemons)
1/2 cup tahini (sesame paste)
1 1/2 tablespoons virgin or extra virgin olive oil
salt, to taste
sprig of flat-leaf parsley, to garnish
paprika, to garnish

Rinse the chickpeas. Place in a saucepan, cover with fresh cold water and boil for 2 hours (or 20 minutes in a pressure cooker). Drain, reserving some of the cooking liquid.

Puree the chickpeas in a food processor, adding enough of the reserved cooking liquid to thin down the puree. Add the garlic, lemon juice, tahini and 1 tablespoon of the olive oil. Mix well and season with salt to taste. Transfer to an airtight plastic container, then spoon over sufficient of the remaining olive oil to just barely cover the surface (this stops the hummus drying out). Seal and refrigerate until you are ready to use.

Serve in a small, shallow bowl, drizzle over a little olive oil and garnish with a sprig of parsley. Sprinkle with paprika. Hummus freezes well, so store any leftovers in a suitable sealed container in the freezer.

Note: Add 1/4 teaspoon of ground cumin for a subtle difference in flavour.

David's Easy Hummus

Serves 6

My eldest son, David, is rather an expert at making this delicious dip and until recently he made the traditional recipe using dried chickpeas. He now opts for this quicker version.

1 x 300 g can of chickpeas
3 cloves garlic, peeled and crushed
juice of 2 fresh lemons (about 4 tablespoons)
$1/3$–$1/2$ cup tahini (sesame paste)
salt, to taste
1 tablespoon olive oil
paprika, to garnish
sprig of fresh parsley, to garnish
Lebanese or Turkish bread, for serving

Open the can of chickpeas then tip into a food processor, including about half the liquid from can (reserve remainder). Add the garlic, lemon juice, tahini, a good pinch of salt and olive oil. Process until smooth and creamy. Thin down with a little more of the reserved liquid (or use olive oil or water), then taste and add extra salt if needed. Put into a serving bowl, drizzle with a little olive oil, then sprinkle with the paprika. Garnish with a sprig of bright green parsley. Serve with bread for dunking.

GUACAMOLE

Makes about 1½ cups

2 ripe avocados
1 level tablespoon finely grated white onion
small clove garlic, crushed (optional)
salt and freshly ground black pepper, to taste
dash of chilli sauce or Tabasco
squeeze of lemon juice

Halve the avocados, then remove stones and skin. Mash the avocado flesh with a fork or smooth out with a food processor. Transfer the avocado puree to a mixing bowl, then mix in the onion and garlic (if using). Season to taste with salt and pepper, and add the chilli sauce. Add a tiny squeeze of lemon juice to help preserve the colour (*too* much lemon can swamp the delicate flavour of the avocados). Cover with plastic wrap until ready to serve (best within an hour). Serve as a dip for corn chips, crisp-baked potato skins, vegetable crudites or prawns.

Note: Peeled, de-seeded and finely chopped tomato is often stirred into guacamole. The tomato tastes good, but it spoils the pristine green colour. A better idea is decorate the dip with chopped tomato when serving.

Baked Ricotta with Gremolata

This little dome of ricotta looks pretty and tastes marvellous.

750 g fresh ricotta
½ cup firmly packed chopped fresh parsley
2 cloves garlic, crushed
2 teaspoons olive oil
grated rind 1 lemon

Press the ricotta firmly into a large sieve, then cover the top of the ricotta with a small plate and put something heavy on it to weight it down. Suspend the sieve over a bowl to drain, then refrigerate overnight or for 24 hours.

Preheat the oven to 180°C (350°F). Turn the dome of ricotta onto a flat ovenproof plate (it spreads in the oven, so make sure the plate is large enough). For the gremolata topping, mix the parsley, garlic, olive oil and lemon rind together. Spread over the top of the ricotta dome. Cover loosely with an ovenproof bowl or a tent of foil (this preserves the pretty green colour). Bake in the oven for about 30 minutes, then remove the covering and cook for a further 10 minutes, or until the ricotta feels set. Cool, then refrigerate until firm. Serve as an antipasto with crusty bread and olives. Other accompaniments could be char-grilled vegetables (zucchini, eggplant and capsicum) or a fresh tomato salsa.

Eggs Benedict

Serves 2–4

4 fresh eggs (as fresh as possible)
2 muffins, split open, or thickly sliced toast
4 slices ham
butter
Hollandaise Sauce (see following)

Poach the eggs in an egg poacher or, if the eggs are very fresh, poach in boiling, salted water (see hints following). Toast and butter the muffins and put onto warm serving dishes. Heat the ham in a little butter in a pan (or in a microwave) and place on the muffins. Top with the hot poached eggs and spoon over the warm Hollandaise Sauce. Serve immediately with chopped chives and ground black pepper.

Hints on Poaching Eggs: Half-fill a frying pan or shallow saucepan with hot water, then heat until boiling. Add a good pinch of salt, then add the eggs, one at a time (carefully break the eggs onto a saucer first, taking care not to break the yolk, then slide the egg off the saucer into water). Cook until the whites are set, 3–4 minutes. Remove the poached eggs from water with a flat perforated or slotted spoon. Let spoon rest for 20 seconds on a folded cloth or paper towel to drain away any excess water.

Microwave Hollandaise Sauce

Serves 4

So easy, you won't believe it.

90 g butter
2 egg yolks
1 tablespoon water
1 tablespoon fresh lemon juice

Put the butter into a small, shallow microwave-safe bowl. Microwave on high to melt the butter (30–45 seconds). Remove the bowl, add the egg yolks, water and lemon juice, and beat well using a small whisk. Microwave on high for 20 seconds, then stop the cooking and whisk well. Set the microwave to defrost and microwave for about 45 seconds, *stopping the oven and whisking every 15 seconds.* Remove from the oven and whisk furiously until the sauce combines and is thick and smooth.

Note: If the sauce seems too thin, microwave for a further 10–20 seconds, stopping to whisk halfway through. The sauce can curdle if overcooked, so it is best to be cautious.

No microwave?
Here's the traditional method. Put the water and lemon juice into a small, heatproof basin. Add the egg yolks and whisk well. Place over *gently* simmering water and whisk until the sauce starts to thicken slightly. Add the melted butter drop by drop, whisking all the time until the sauce is thick and creamy. Remove from the heat and season with salt and a few drops of extra lemon juice if necessary.

Fluffy Scrambled Eggs

Serves 2

These scrambled eggs are light and fluffy, and not too rich.

4 eggs
½ cup milk
tiny pinch of salt
1 level tablespoon butter
hot, buttered toast
fresh chives or parsley, chopped
freshly ground black pepper, to taste

Beat the eggs and milk together and season lightly with salt. Melt the butter in a small, heavy-based (preferably nonstick) saucepan, then add the egg mixture and stir gently with a wooden spoon. Cook over a very low heat, stirring often, until the eggs start to set around the edges, then put a lid on the pan for just a minute or so (this makes the eggs light and fluffy, but please don't walk away and leave it because overcooked scrambled eggs are disappointing). The trick is to stop the cooking while the mixture is still creamy and a touch under-cooked, as with an omelette. The mixture will finish cooking almost as you are serving it. Pile quickly onto hot, buttered toast and smother with chives (a tiny pinch of dried rosemary is good, too) and plenty of pepper.

Hint: If you should overcook the scrambled egg, you can save it by quickly stirring in another beaten egg mixed with a little milk or cream.

Puddings

Lemon Pancakes
Apple and Blackcurrant Trifle
Baked Apricot Jam Roly
Golden Syrup Dumplings
Lemon Delicious
Crème Brûlée
Vanilla Egg Custard
Boiled Vanilla Custard
Panna Cotta
Gwen's Upside-down Pear Cake
Bread and Butter Pudding
Steamed Marmalade Pudding
Creamy Rice Pudding
French Caramel Apple Pudding
Apple Crumble
Apple Pie
Banana Fritters
Rhubarb and Apple
Summer Fruit Salad

Lemon Pancakes

Serves 4

Gathering in the kitchen eagerly devouring pancakes hot from the pan is a happy memory for most of us ... Remember how even the mistakes and broken ones were never wasted?

1½ cups self-raising flour
pinch of salt
¼ cup caster sugar
2 eggs
2 tablespoons melted butter
1 ¾ cups (435 mL) milk
½ teaspoon vanilla essence
butter for cooking
juice of 4 lemons
extra sugar for sprinkling

Sift the flour, salt and sugar into a mixing bowl. Make a well in the centre and break in the eggs. Add the butter and one cup of milk. Beat well to smooth out any lumps, then add the remaining milk and the vanilla essence.

Before you start to cook the pancakes, put a large saucepan half-filled with water on to boil. Place a heat-proof plate over the boiling water. (This will keep the pancakes hot as you cook them.)

Heat a little dot of butter in a frying pan or a 15 cm (6 in) crêpe pan and when sizzling hot, pour in some batter (allow 3 tablespoons for an average-sized pan or 2 tablespoons for a crêpe pan). Twist the pan quickly so the batter covers the base, then pour away any excess. Cook on a high heat until golden underneath, then turn over with a spatula to cook *very briefly* on the other side.

As the pancakes cook, stack them on the plate over the saucepan, sprinkling each one with a good squeeze of lemon juice and a little sugar as you go. When all are cooked, roll up and serve immediately.

Apple and Blackcurrant Trifle

Serves 8

2 packets of blackcurrant jelly
3 large cooking apples, peeled, cored and thickly sliced
½ cup (125 mL) water
¼ cup plus 1 tablespoon sugar
pinch of ground cloves
3 level tablespoons custard powder
3 cups (750mL) milk
1 thin strip lemon rind (remove from lemon with a potato peeler)
2 teaspoons vanilla essence
1¼ cups (300 mL) thickened cream, lightly whipped
1 x 20 cm sponge cake
¼ cup (65mL) sweet sherry
grated nutmeg
¼ cup Vienna almonds, chopped

Make the jellies according to the instructions on the packet and pour into a square container. Chill until set, then cut into cubes.

Simmer the apples in the water with the 1 tablespoon sugar and cloves, then allow to cool. Put the custard powder into a saucepan, stir in a small quantity of the milk, then smooth out with a wooden spoon. Add the remaining milk, the ¼ cup sugar and lemon peel. Stir over a medium heat until the custard boils and thickens. Reduce the heat and cook for a further minute or so, stirring often, then add the vanilla essence. Pour the custard into a bowl and, when cool, remove the lemon peel and fold the cream through the custard (this produces a beautiful consistency).

Break the sponge cake into large pieces, then put half in the bottom of a serving dish. Sprinkle with half of the sherry, then add the apples. Pour over half the custard, add another layer of sherried sponge and finish with a layer of custard. Sprinkle lightly with the nutmeg. Cover with plastic wrap and refrigerate for an hour or two for the flavours to mingle.

Just before serving, sprinkle over the Vienna almonds and add the chopped jelly. Accompany with a bowl of whipped cream.

BAKED APRICOT JAM ROLY

Serves 4

Remember how the syrup formed a toffee on the sides of this dish? What a prize it was to be the chosen child to clean off that toffee?

---

1 cup self-raising flour
50g butter or margarine
¼ cup cold water
1 heaped tablespoon apricot conserve
½ cup sultanas

Syrup
1 (250 mL) cup water
½ cup sugar
50 g butter or margarine
thin strip of lemon peel
1 level tablespoon sugar, for topping

Preheat the oven to 180°C (350°F). Sift the flour into a mixing bowl. Rub in the butter, then add the water and mix quickly into a dough. Roll out thinly on a floured surface to a rectangular shape. Spread with the apricot conserve then sprinkle with the sultanas. Roll the dough up from the longest side, Swiss roll fashion, and place into a greased casserole dish, easing roll around to fit the shape of the dish.

To make the syrup, put the water, sugar, butter and lemon peel into a saucepan and bring to the boil. Pour over the pastry roll, discarding the peel. Make a few slits here and there in the dough, then sprinkle over the extra sugar (for a crunchy top). Bake, uncovered, in the oven for about 35–45 minutes.

Serve with lots of homemade Boiled Vanilla Custard (see page 123).

Apple Roly: Spread the pastry with raspberry jam instead of apricot conserve then grate over 2 large Granny Smith apples. Roll the dough up and continue as in recipe above.

Golden Syrup Dumplings

Serves 4

1⅓ cups (330 mL) water
½ cup sugar
2 level tablespoons golden syrup
2 teaspoons fresh lemon juice
30 g butter

Dumplings
1 cup self-raising flour
30 g butter
1 egg
1–1½ tablespoons milk

Put the water, sugar, golden syrup, lemon juice and butter into a wide shallow saucepan over a low heat. Stir occasionally to dissolve the sugar.

Meanwhile, make the dumplings. Sift the flour into a mixing bowl. Rub in the butter. Make a well in the centre and add the egg and milk. Mix gently, just enough to combine the ingredients (don't mix too much). Form into little balls with floured hands or alternatively drop from a spoon into the boiling syrup. Cover the pan immediately with a lid (this is the most important step — steam is necessary for fluffy dumplings). Reduce the heat and simmer until the dumplings are cooked and well risen, about 6–10 minutes, depending on size. Don't overcook or they will be tough. Serve immediately with cream or Boiled Vanilla Custard (see page 123).

Lemon Delicious

Serves 6

This Australian family pudding, has been much loved for generations for the way it forms a delicate lemon cake with a smooth sauce underneath. That sauce was always in demand (there never seemed to be enough in the baking dish to go around)! This updated version is baked in individual dishes, so that everyone has their own creamy lemon sauce.

½ cup self-raising flour
¾ cup caster sugar
finely grated rind 1 lemon
¼ cup fresh lemon juice
4 tablespoons melted butter
3 eggs, separated
1¼ cups (315 mL) milk

Preheat the oven to 180°C (350°F). Lightly grease six ¾-cup individual soufflé dishes (5–6 cm deep) or one 1.5 litre ovenproof dish (6 cm) deep.

Put the flour, sugar and lemon rind into a mixing bowl. Make a well in the centre, then add the lemon juice, melted butter and egg yolks. Beat with a wooden spoon to mix, then gradually stir in the milk to make a batter.

In a separate large mixing bowl, whisk the egg whites until stiff and white. Gradually pour the lemon batter into the egg whites. Fold through lightly until well mixed. Divide the mixture *evenly* between the individual dishes (stir the mixture in the bowl every now and then to prevent it separating into layers). The mixture doesn't rise too much so the dishes can be filled up to 1 cm from the top. (Alternatively, pour the mixture into the large bowl.) Put in a large baking dish with sufficient cold water to come halfway up the sides of the dishes. Bake in the oven for about 40–45 minutes for individual puddings or 1 hour for the large one. Cover large pudding loosely with foil if it browns too much. Serve warm with a little pouring cream or with vanilla ice cream.

Passionfruit Delicious: To make this version, omit the lemon rind and juice and add instead ⅓–½ cup of passionfruit pulp (this is usually the pulp of 4–6 large passionfruit).

Crème Brûlée

Serves 6

1 egg
4 egg yolks
¾ cup caster sugar
1½ cups cream
1¼ cups milk
1 teaspoon vanilla essence
fresh fruit, for serving

Preheat the oven to 160°C (325°F). Break the egg into a mixing bowl, then add the egg yolks and ¼ cup of the sugar. Whisk together immediately (see note). Heat the cream and milk in a saucepan until scalding hot, then pour onto the eggs, whisking constantly until well mixed and the sugar is dissolved. Strain into a jug, then pour into six ½-cup souffle dishes (they should be almost filled to the top). Put into a baking dish with sufficient water to come halfway up the sides of the dishes. Bake in the oven for 45 minutes, or until they are 'wobbly' set. Remove from the oven and allow the custards to cool (out of the baking dish) for about 20 minutes before refrigerating immediately.

Using a small tea strainer, evenly sieve 1 tablespoon of the remaining caster sugar over each of the chilled custards. Wipe any sugar off the rims of the dishes (this tends to burn). Heat a griller until it is very hot (a gas griller is ideal for this), then place one or two custards at a time under the griller, close to the heat, until the sugar melts into a golden toffee (don't take your eyes off them, it takes just a matter of minutes). If the toffee starts to burn, spray with a little water *(and be careful to protect your hands to avoid burning yourself)*. When all the toppings are done, cool the custards, then return to the refrigerator until ready to serve.

To serve, put each souffle dish of crème brûlée onto a serving plate and accompany with fresh fruit such as raspberries, strawberries, grapes, slivered mango or sweet orange segments. The idea is for guests to smash the toffee gently with a serving spoon, then dig into the smooth vanilla cream.

Brûlée Surprise: Try putting some fresh raspberries or strawberries in the bottom of the souffle dish before pouring in the custard.

Note: If you sprinkle sugar onto egg yolks then leave them to stand, it tends to 'harden' the yolks. So always whisk sugar through immediately.

Vanilla Egg Custard

Serves 4–6

Serve warm with fresh summer berries or as a chilled sauce with mixed berries or poached stone fruit, or with baked pastries and puddings.

1½ cups milk
½ cup cream
thin strip of fresh lemon peel
piece of vanilla bean (optional)
4 egg yolks
¼ cup raw or crystal sugar
½ teaspoon vanilla extract or 1 teaspoon vanilla essence

Heat the milk and cream slowly with the lemon peel and vanilla bean (if using). When the liquid is almost boiling, remove from the heat and leave to infuse for 5 minutes.

Meanwhile, put the egg yolks into a small mixing bowl, then add the sugar and whisk well. Pour some of the hot milk mixture onto the yolks, whisking all the time, then return this mixture to the saucepan.

Cook over a *very low heat,* stirring constantly with a wooden spoon in a figure eight movement, until the custard leaves the trace of your finger on the back of the spoon. Remove from the heat and discard the lemon peel and the vanilla bean. Boost the flavour with the vanilla extract. (The custard may look thin compared to thickened custards, but that is how it is meant to be.) Serve warm. If serving cold, pour into a jug and put plastic wrap right down on the surface of the custard to prevent a skin forming. Refrigerate until ready to serve.

Boiled Vanilla Custard

Makes 2½ cups

2½ cups (600 mL) milk
¼ cup sugar
thin strip of lemon rind (pare a thin strip of rind with a potato peeler)
2 level tablespoons custard powder
2 egg yolks (optional)
1 teaspoon vanilla essence

Put 2 cups of the milk into a saucepan with the sugar and lemon rind. Bring slowly to simmering point. Meanwhile, mix the custard powder with the remaining ½ cup milk. Stir into the simmering milk. Stir constantly until the custard boils and thickens.

Mix the egg yolks (if using) and vanilla in a small mixing bowl. Tip a little of the hot custard into the bowl, mix quickly, then pour back into the saucepan. Turn off the heat and whisk the custard thoroughly (the heat of the custard is sufficient to cook the yolks). Discard the lemon peel and thin the custard, if necessary, with a little extra milk or cream.

Serve hot or warm over puddings and pies, or with stewed fruit. If serving cold, pour into a basin and cover tightly with plastic wrap (right down onto the surface to preven a skin forming) and refrigerate until ready to use.

Panna Cotta

Serves 4

A smooth vanilla cream with a melt-in-the-mouth consistency. Fruit in season is the perfect accompaniment.

1¼ cups (300 mL) cream
⅔ cup (150 mL) milk
¼ cup sugar
¼ cup boiling water
2 level teaspoons gelatine
2 teaspoons vanilla essence or 1 teaspoon vanilla extract
fruit in season, fresh or poached

Put the cream, milk and sugar into a heavy-based saucepan. Heat gently until almost boiling, stirring often to make sure the sugar is dissolved. Remove from the heat. Pour the boiling water into a cup, then add the gelatine and whisk with a fork until completely dissolved. Add to the cream mixture with the vanilla essence. Pour into a jug to cool slightly, but cover with food plastic right down onto the surface so the cream doesn't form a skin.

When cooled to lukewarm, give it a good stir then pour into four small (½ cup) moulds. Put onto a tray, then cover loosely with plastic wrap and refrigerate until set, usually about 4 hours. There is just enough gelatine in this cream to barely set the Panna Cotta, but don't be tempted to increase the quantity except during heat wave conditions as this would spoil the consistency. Turn out just before serving.

To turn out, dip moulds *briefly* into warm water to loosen, then turn out onto serving plates. Serve with poached quinces, peaches, nectarines or plums, and drizzle with the fruit's cooking syrup. Alternatively, serve with fresh fruit in season (strawberries, raspberries, figs, blueberries or orange segments) and pour over a little Caramel Syrup (see page following) or maple syrup.

Note: During heatwave conditions, increase gelatine to 2½ level teaspoons.

Caramel Syrup

Makes about ¾ cup

½ cup sugar
¼ cup (65 mL) plus an extra ½ cup (125 mL) water
2–3 teaspoons liqueur (such as Cointreau, Grand Marnier or Mandarine Napoleon)

Put the sugar and water into a saucepan. Stir over a low heat until all the sugar dissolves. Brush down the sides of the pan with a wet pastry brush to ensure all the sugar crystals are dissolved. Remove the spoon and boil the syrup until it is a pale golden colour (don't walk away and leave it, caramel can burn quickly). Remove from the heat immediately. Wrap a cloth around your hands (or wear protective gloves) and, *holding the pan at arm's length,* pour in an additional ½ cup water. The caramel bubbles up and is very hot, *so stand safely back*. Return the caramel to the heat to dissolve any toffee in the bottom of pan, then cool and add the liqueur. Store in the refrigerator where it will keep for 5 days.

Gwen's Upside-down Pear Cake

Serves 6–8

60g butter
⅓ cup lightly packed brown sugar
1 x 425 g can pear halves, well drained

Ginger Sponge
1 cup self-raising flour
¼ level teaspoon bi-carb soda
1 level teaspoon ground ginger
1 level teaspoon ground cinnamon
½ level teaspoon ground cloves
½ cup caster sugar
2 level tablespoons butter
2 level tablespoons golden syrup
2 large eggs
½ cup (125 mL) milk

Preheat oven to 170°–180°C (325°–350°F). Grease well with butter a 20 x 5 cm (8 x 2 in) round nonstick cake tin.

Cream the butter and brown sugar together, then spread evenly over the base of the prepared cake tin. Arrange the pear halves in a pattern on top of the creamed mixture, then set aside while making the ginger sponge.

To make the ginger sponge, sift the flour, bi-carb soda, ginger, cinnamon and cloves into a mixing bowl. Add the caster sugar, mix through, then make a well in the centre. Melt the butter with the golden syrup, then pour into the well with the eggs and milk. Beat well with a wooden spoon (this is a thin batter). Pour over the pears in the tin, then bake in the oven for 1–1¼ hours. Test by inserting a fine skewer into the middle of the cake. If it comes out clean, the cake is cooked. Remove from the oven and let stand for 5–10 minutes. Loosen the cake from sides of tin with a spatula, then turn out carefully onto a flat plate. Cut into wedges and serve warm as a dessert cake with thick cream or custard.

Bread and Butter Pudding

Serves 4–6

5 eggs
½ cup sugar
3 cups milk
1 teaspoon vanilla essence
1 heaped tablespoon sultanas
4 slices white bread, lightly buttered with crusts removed
pouring cream, for serving
fresh or stewed fruit, for serving

Preheat the oven to 160°C (325°F). Break the eggs into a mixing bowl, then add the sugar and whisk together lightly. Add the milk and vanilla essence, and whisk through. Pour into a lightly buttered ovenproof dish (about 5 cup capacity), then add the sultanas. Cut the buttered bread into fingers or triangles then float, buttered side up, on the custard, overlapping the bread here and there (any high peaks on the bread are extra crunchy).

Put the dish into a larger baking dish with sufficient cold water to come halfway up the side of the dish. Bake in the oven for $1^1/_2$–2 hours, or until the topping is golden and crisp on the edges and the custard is set. Before removing from the oven, test by inserting a small knife in the centre; if the custard is still runny, cook a little longer.

Serve warm with a little pouring cream and accompany with fresh fruit (strawberries or sweetened raspberries are especially good) or stewed fruit such as apples, rhubarb, quinces, nectarines or plums.

Steamed Marmalade Pudding

Serves 6

½ cup sweet orange marmalade
125 g butter
½ cup caster sugar
grated rind of 1 orange
2 eggs
1½ cups self-raising flour, sifted
¼ cup (65 mL) fresh orange juice
¼ cup (65 mL) milk
2 tablespoons Grand Marnier or Cointreau
Boiled Vanilla Custard (see page 123), for serving

Grease a 1.5 litre pudding basin well with butter, then put a small round of baking paper in the bottom (as a precaution against sticking). Spoon the marmalade into the bottom of the basin and set aside while making the pudding.

Cream the butter, sugar and orange rind until light and fluffy. Add the eggs one at a time, beating well after each addition. Add the sifted flour and stir in lightly, then add the orange juice and milk. Give the mixture a good beat for a few seconds, then put into the basin on top of the marmalade. Cover with baking paper (cut to fit the top of basin), then with two sheets of foil. Tie securely with string. Lower into a big saucepan of boiling water (sufficient to come two-thirds up the side of the basin). Cover the saucepan and simmer for 1¼–1½ hours. Remove the pudding basin from the saucepan immediately and let stand for 5 minutes. Using a small spatula, check that the side of the pudding is not catching on the basin. Turn out onto a large plate. Pour the liqueur over the top, then cut into wedges and serve with lots of homemade Vanilla Custard.

Golden Syrup Pudding: Use ½ cup golden syrup instead of marmalade.

Raspberry Pudding: Use raspberry jam instead of marmalade. Cream the butter and sugar with 1 teaspoon vanilla essence, and omit the orange rind. Replace the orange juice and milk mixture with ½ cup milk and the orange liqueur with Kirsch.

Creamy Rice Pudding

Serves 6

The trick to making really creamy rice is knowing when to stop the cooking.

½ cup short-grain rice
⅓ cup sugar
4 cups (1 litre) milk
¼ cup (65 mL) cream (optional)
1 heaped teaspoon butter (optional)
grated nutmeg

Preheat the oven to 130°–150°C (275°–300°F). Put the rice, sugar, milk and cream into a deep ovenproof dish (such as a casserole). Bake in the oven for about 2–2½ hours. While the rice is cooking, stir it from time to time. If you like the golden skin on top (some say it's the best part), leave the pudding undisturbed during the last 45 minutes of cooking and dot with butter. The rice is ready when the milk is the consistency of thickened cream and the rice is plump and creamy. Please don't overcook, so that it sticks together in a solid lump (if this should happen, simply stir in some cream until the pudding is the right consistency). Sprinkle very lightly with a little grated nutmeg. Serve warm with stewed, new season apples or a compote of dried fruits.

FRENCH CARAMEL APPLE PUDDING

Serves 8

A light cake topping baked over apples in caramel sauce.

Caramel
¾ cup sugar
4 tablespoons water

Apples
1 kg Granny Smith cooking apples
½ cup water
2 level tablespoons sugar
3 whole cloves

Cake Topping
100 g butter or margarine
½ cup caster sugar
1 teaspoon vanilla essence
2 eggs
¾ cup self-raising flour, sifted
2 tablespoons milk
icing sugar and vanilla ice cream or thick cream for serving

The first step is to put a 6-cup (1.5 litre) ovenproof dish (4–5 cm deep) by the side of the stove in readiness (you will see the wisdom of this as you proceed).

Preheat the oven to 180°–190°C (350°–375°F). To make the caramel, put the sugar into a saucepan, then add the 4 tablespoons water. Stir over a low heat until the sugar dissolves. Brush the sides of the saucepan with a wet pastry brush to remove any sugar crystals (these can cause the syrup to candy). When the sugar has dissolved, remove the spoon and boil the syrup rapidly over a high heat until it is a pale golden colour. Pour *immediately* into the ovenproof dish so it completely covers the base.

Peel, quarter and core the apples, then cut into thick wedges. Put into a saucepan with the ½ cup water, sugar and cloves. Simmer gently for about 10 minutes, until the apples are tender but still retain their shape. Turn off the heat but leave the apples in the saucepan.

While the apples are cooking, make the cake topping. Cream the butter, caster sugar and vanilla essence until light and fluffy, then add the eggs one at a time, beating well after each addition. Stir in the flour, then add the milk and mix lightly. Reheat the apples if necessary (this is important, see Note), then pour the apples and all the liquid from the saucepan into the caramel-lined dish, discarding the cloves. Cover the *hot* apples immediately with the cake topping and bake in the oven for 45-50 minutes, or until the cake is cooked through (test in the centre with a fine skewer). Serve while warm and still crusty on top. Accompany with vanilla ice cream, which will melt deliciously over the pudding. It is also good with thick cream, homemade vanilla custard or custard yoghurt.

Note: The apples should be *hot* when adding the cake topping so that the cake will cook sufficiently underneath that is the golden rule when cooking this style of pudding.

Apple Crumble

Serves 4

6 large Granny Smith apples, peeled, cored and quartered
¾ cup water
1 tablespoon sugar
few cloves (optional)

Crumble Topping
½ cup self-raising flour
100 g butter
½ cup lightly packed brown sugar
½ cup rolled oats or desiccated coconut

Preheat the oven to 180°C (350°F). Cut the apple into thick slices, then put into a saucepan with the water, sugar and cloves (if using). Cook until the apples are tender. Discard the cloves, then pour the apples and all the cooking syrup into a shallow ovenproof dish.

    To make the crumble topping, put the flour into a mixing bowl and rub in the butter. Add the brown sugar and rolled oats, and mix through. Arrange the crumble in little heaps over the apples (it joins together during cooking). Bake in the oven for about 30 minutes. Serve warm or cold with thick cream, vanilla ice cream or homemade vanilla custard.

Apple Pie

Serves 8

1.5 kg Granny Smith apples (7–8 large apples), peeled, cored and sliced
1 cup (250 mL) water
a few whole cloves
¼ cup caster sugar
1 level tablespoon plain flour
Crunchy Shortcrust Pastry (recipe following)

Preheat oven to 200°–210°C (400°–425°F). Put the apples into a large saucepan with the water and cloves. Cover with a lid and simmer over a low heat for about 10 minutes, or until the apples are soft but not broken. Drain into a colander and leave until cold. Remove the cloves then press the apples gently in the colander to remove any excess liquid (reserve the apple liquid to glaze the pie). Put the apples into a mixing bowl, add the sugar and flour and mix.

Roll out half the pastry (not too thinly) to fit a 22 cm fluted metal pie plate or flan tin (3.5 cm deep) with a removable base. Place the pastry-lined tin on a sturdy baking tray, then fill with the apple mixture, piling up in the middle. Roll out the remaining pastry and cover the pie (wet the edges where the pastry joins). Trim away any excess pastry, then press the edges together with a fork. Brush the pie with some of the reserved apple liquid. Sprinkle evenly with 1 level tablespoon additional sugar (for a crunchy topping). Bake in the oven for about 1 hour. Serve warm, with thick cream.

Crunchy Shortcrust Pastry

1 cup plain flour
1 cup self-raising flour
½ level teaspoon salt
150 g butter
¼ cup caster sugar
1 egg
2–3 teaspoons cold or iced water

Sift the plain flour, self-raising flour and salt into a mixing bowl. Rub in the butter then add the sugar. Make a well in the centre, break the egg into the well, then add the cold or iced water. Mix quickly into a dough and knead lightly.

BANANA FRITTERS

Serves 6

1 cup self-raising flour
¾ cup plus 1 tablespoon water
1 tablespoon light vegetable oil
1 egg white, stiffly beaten
6 large bananas
2 level tablespoons plain flour
light vegetable oil, for deep-frying
icing sugar, for dusting
lemon wedges, for serving
whipped cream or vanilla ice cream, for serving

Sift the self-raising flour into a mixing bowl, make a well in the centre, then add the ¾ cup of water and oil, and beat until smooth. Fold in the egg white, then lighten the batter with the extra 1 tablespoon water.

Peel and halve the bananas, then dust lightly with the plain flour. Coat the bananas with the batter, then deep-fry in hot oil for a few minutes, until they're crisp and golden. Drain immediately on crumpled paper towels. Shake some icing sugar through a small strainer over the bananas, then serve immediately with lemon wedges and whipped cream or vanilla ice cream.

Rhubarb and Apple

Serves 6

3 cooking apples, peeled, cored and quartered
1 cup (250 mL) water
1 bunch of rhubarb (20 large sticks or 4 cups chopped homegrown rhubarb)
1 level teaspoon finely grated orange rind
½ cup sugar

Cut the apples into thick slices and put in a saucepan with the water. Simmer, loosely covered, for 10 minutes.

Meanwhile, remove and discard the rhubarb leaves (see Note). Wash the red rhubarb sticks, then chop into 5 cm pieces. When the apple is almost cooked, add the rhubarb, orange rind and sugar. Return to the boil and simmer uncovered for 3–5 minutes (try not to overcook; the rhubarb should retain its shape). Pour into a dish and refrigerate. Serve with lots of homemade Boiled Vanilla Custard (see page 123).

Note: Always discard the leaves of rhubarb since they are mildly poisonous.

Rhubarb Crumble: Pour the rhubarb and apple mixture into a shallow ovenproof dish then arrange Crumble Topping (see page 132) over the top in little heaps. Bake in a moderate oven (180°C/350°F) for about 30 minutes. Serve warm with thick cream, vanilla or coconut ice cream, or custard.

Summer Fruit Salad

Serves 6–8

Nobody feels like cooking in the heat of summer, let alone turning on the oven to bake a desert. This very easy compote of summer fruits is easy to put together, especially when entertaining a crowd, and everyone seems to love the abundance of berries.

2 punnets strawberries
1 punnet raspberries
1 punnet blueberries
1 mango
3 passionfruit
juice of 1 orange
1 level tablespoon sugar
1 tablespoon Grand Marnier or Kirsch
2 level tablespoons icing sugar
some strawberry, mulberry or citrus leaves, for decoration

Wash the strawberries, then remove the green hulls. Tumble the strawberries, raspberries and blueberries onto a large platter. Cut the mango flesh into small chunks, then scatter it over the berries. Scoop the passionfruit pulp into a small basin; add orange juice, sugar and liqueur, mix well to dissolve the sugar, then drizzle over the fruit. Sift over the icing sugar, garnish with a few green leaves and serve with thick cream or a good vanilla ice cream.

Biscuits, Cakes and Slices

Anzac Biscuits
Chocolate Chip Biscuits
My Favourite Gingerbread Biscuits
Jam Drops
Joy's Melting Moments
Almond Friands
Double Chocolate Cake
Carrot Cake in a Baking Dish
Lemon Sauce Cake
Orange and Almond Cake
Cream Scones
Chocolate Slice
Walnut Crescents

Anzac Biscuits

Makes 4 dozen

These 'Anzacs' are especially light and crunchy, with a delicious homemade flavour.

---

1 cup plain flour
2 level teaspoons ground ginger
1 cup rolled oats
1 cup desiccated coconut
¾ cup caster sugar
150 g butter or margarine
1 level tablespoon golden syrup
1 level teaspoon bicarbonate of soda
2 tablespoons cold water

Preheat the oven to 170°C (325°F). Grease baking trays well with butter and line with baking paper (see Note).

Sift the flour and ginger into a mixing bowl, then add the rolled oats, coconut and sugar, and mix together. Melt the butter and golden syrup in a small saucepan over a low heat (or in a microwave-safe dish in the microwave on full power for about 60 seconds). Put the bicarbonate of soda into a small dish, crush any lumps with a teaspoon then mix in the cold water. Add this to the melted butter and syrup, then pour into the dry ingredients and mix with a wooden spoon.

Put rounded teaspoons of the mixture onto the trays, leaving plenty of room for spreading (they should be at least 5 cm apart). Flatten slightly with a spatula, then bake in the oven for about 20 minutes. After removing the biscuits from oven, leave them to firm up for a few minutes before removing them from the trays with a metal spatula. When quite cold, store in an airtight container.

Note: If you omit the baking paper, make sure that you grease the trays well. Anzacs become very crisp as they cool, so remove or loosen while still warm to prevent shattering.

Sultana Anzacs: Mix in 3 tablespoons sultanas with the dry ingredients. When baked, the Anzacs will have a nice little surprise of juicy fruit here and there.

Chocolate Chip Biscuits

Makes about 50

These delicious little biscuits are studded with toasted hazelnuts and chocolate chips.

250 g butter or margarine
1 cup firmly packed brown sugar
1 teaspoon vanilla essence
1 egg
1½ cups self-raising flour, sifted
½ cup plain flour, sifted
½ cup desiccated coconut
125 g (1 cup) toasted hazelnuts, chopped (see below)
100 g dark chocolate, chopped

Preheat the oven to 190°C (375°F). Grease several baking trays well with butter.
    Cream the butter, brown sugar and vanilla essence, then beat in the egg. Mix in the sifted flours, coconut, hazelnuts and chocolate. Roll the mixture into small balls using floured hands (add 1 extra tablespoon of flour if the mixture sticks to your hands). Place onto the prepared trays, leaving room between to allow for spreading. There is no need to flatten the biscuits, as they will spread more evenly if left alone. Bake in the oven for about 20 minutes. Loosen from the trays while still warm; these biscuits are very crisp and could shatter if allowed to cool on the trays without loosening (alternatively, line the trays with baking paper). When cold, store in an airtight container.

Toasted Hazelnuts: Put the hazelnuts into a cake tin and toast in a moderately slow oven (160°C/325°F) for 20 minutes, then rub off the brown papery skins with a tea towel (don't worry if some skin remains).

My Favourite Gingerbread Biscuits

Makes 36 gingerbread men or 60 stars

My grandchildren adore these biscuits and request them every year for their birthday parties with specific instructions on the shape. Gingerbread men, hearts or stars seem to be the most popular, but depending on the latest craze, they can also be almost anything from dinosaurs to fairies.

150 g butter or margarine
3 level tablespoons golden syrup
¾ cup caster sugar
2 cups plain flour
1 cup self-raising flour
1 level teaspoon bicarbonate of soda
1 level teaspoon ground cinnamon
1 level teaspoon ground ginger
½ level teaspoon ground cloves
1 egg
1 egg yolk
1 teaspoon vanilla essence

Preheat oven to 190°C (375°F). Lightly grease several flat baking trays and line with baking paper.

Put the butter, golden syrup and sugar into a saucepan. Heat to dissolve, then cool to lukewarm.

Sift the plain flour, self-raising flour, bicarbonate of soda, cinnamon, ginger and cloves into a mixing bowl. Mix well together, then make a well in the middle. Add the egg, egg yolk, vanilla essence and lukewarm syrup mixture. Mix thoroughly, then take about one-third of the mixture at a time and knead lightly (preferably while still warm) using a little flour. Dust a flat surface with a little flour (not too much) then roll out *firmly* using a floured rolling pin. Cut out with fancy cutters.

Arrange the gingerbread shapes on the prepared trays, leaving just a little between them for spreading. Bake in the oven for 10–12 minutes. The exact cooking time can vary, depending on your oven and the thickness of the biscuits. Remove from the trays to cool on a wire rack, then store in an airtight container. Serve perfectly plain or, for special occasions, such as birthdays and Christmas, decorate with icing.

Note: For adult tastes, make thin spicy biscuits to serve with coffee with the addition of a couple of good pinches of ground cardamom. Roll the mixture very thinly so the biscuits are very crisp then cut out into hearts or stars and bake at 180°C (350°F) for 8–10 minutes. Take care not to overcook the biscuits because they will burn quickly after this time.

Jam Drops

Makes 40

Children love making these biscuits — and eating them, too.

---

125 g butter
½ cup caster sugar
1 teaspoon vanilla essence
1 teaspoon finely grated lemon rind
1 egg
1 cup self-raising flour, sifted
½ cup plain flour, sifted
squeeze of fresh lemon juice
2 level tablespoons strawberry jam

Preheat the oven to 180°C (350°F). Grease several baking trays, and line with baking paper if you wish.

Cream the butter, sugar, vanilla essence and lemon rind, then beat in the egg. Add the sifted flours and mix through, then add a tiny squeeze of lemon juice. Using teaspoons of the mixture, roll into small balls with lightly floured hands (don't make the mistake of making them any bigger than this, because they will spread). Place onto the greased oven trays, leaving room between for spreading. Make a small indent in each one using the pointed end of a egg (this sounds strange, but it is an old country trick and it works beautifully), then fill the hollow with jam. Bake in the oven until a pale golden colour, about 15–20 minutes. Remove from the oven then slide off the trays using a spatula. When cool, pack into an airtight container.

Joy's Melting Moments

Makes 3 dozen (72 single biscuits)

These are really melt-in-the-mouth biscuits.

250 g butter or margarine
1 cup icing sugar mixture
2 teaspoons vanilla essence
2 cups plain flour
½ cup cornflour

Preheat the oven to 180°C (350°F). Grease several baking trays and line with baking paper.
    Cream the butter, icing sugar and vanilla essence together in a mixing bowl, then sift in the flour and cornflour, and mix well. Roll the mixture into small balls and place onto the prepared baking trays. Press down lightly with the tines of a fork (dip the fork into flour first). This mixture is the right consistency to use in a Swedish biscuit press, so if you own one, you may prefer to use it to shape the biscuits. Bake in the oven for 15–20 minutes. Cool and join together with cream filling or leave them as separate little biscuits.

Cream Filling: Beat 75 g butter with 1 cup icing sugar mixture until smooth and creamy, then flavour with few drops of vanilla or lemon essence (or a mixture of both).

Yo Yos: These biscuits are known as yo yos in South Australia when custard powder replaces the cornflour.

ALMOND FRIANDS

Makes 10

A popular little cake in coffee shops and surprisingly easy to make. For best results, purchase some oval moulds and make sure you bake them the day before.

175 g butter
1 cup almond meal
1½ cups sifted pure icing sugar
⅓ cup plus 1 level tablespoon plain flour
5 egg whites
1 level tablespoon very finely chopped blanched almonds

Preheat the oven to 230°C (450°F). Grease 10 oval friand (or pâté) moulds (½ cup capacity) well with butter. You can use ½-cup muffin tins as a substitute.

Put the butter into a saucepan and simmer gently until it just starts to turn golden (this gives a delicate nutty flavour, but don't burn). Set aside to cool slightly.

Meanwhile, put the almond meal, sifted icing sugar and flour into a mixing bowl. Add the unbeaten egg whites and mix together. Pour the warm butter through a strainer into the mixture and mix well, then stir in the almonds.

Spoon the mixture into the friand moulds, filling them no more than three-quarters full. Place the moulds onto a baking tray then bake in the oven for 5 minutes. Reduce the oven temperature to 200°C (400°F) and bake for a further 10–15 minutes. Turn off the heat but leave the cakes in the oven for about 5 minutes before removing. Turn out onto a cake rack to cool.

Put into an airtight container and leave at room temperature overnight before serving. (Friands are better the next day — the crust softens and the cakes become very moist. The flavour is also improved the next day, and is not so sweet.)

Note: Friand moulds are available at gourmet kitchen shops. Many of these shops will post to country customers for a small additional cost to cover postage.

Double Chocolate Cake

125 g pure dark chocolate, chopped
2 tablespoons strong black coffee
125 g butter
½ cup caster sugar
3 large eggs, separated
½ cup almond meal, firmly packed
½ cup plain flour, sifted
1 level tablespoon redcurrant jelly or seedless blackberry conserve

Ganache
75 g pure dark chocolate (or use a mixture of dark and milk chocolate)
50 g unsalted butter, softened to room temperature

Preheat the oven to 180°C (350°F). Grease an 18 or 20 cm sponge sandwich tin and line the base with baking paper.

Melt the chocolate with the coffee in a small pan over a very low heat, stirring often until smooth. Remove from the heat. Cream the butter and sugar until light and fluffy. Add the egg yolks and beat well, then stir in the almond meal and sifted flour.

Whip the egg whites in a separate bowl until they're white and form soft peaks (but not chunky). Fold through the cake mixture with the melted chocolate. Put into the prepared cake tin and bake in the oven for 25–30 minutes. The centre of the cake should still look a little moist when the baking is finished.

Turn the oven off and wedge the door open. Leave the cake a further 5–10 minutes to settle. Remove from the oven and turn out onto a wire rack. Warm the jam in a small saucepan (or in a microwave-safe dish in the microwave for 20 seconds), then spread a layer over the top of the cake. Let the glaze set, then frost the cake all over with the ganache.

To make the ganache, melt the chocolate in a bowl over hot water. Add the soft butter and stir to melt (try not to let any steam or water get into the chocolate). Remove from the hot water and stir occasionally until the mixture starts to thicken. Spread over the cake immediately.

Carrot Cake in a Baking Dish

I used to make this cake a lot when my sons were living at home and the house was always full of hungry teenagers. It's easy make, too, using only a mixing bowl and a wooden spoon.

5 eggs
1¾ cups caster sugar
1½ cups (375 mL) sunflower oil
2 cups plain flour
1 cup self-raising flour
2 level teaspoon bicarbonate of soda
3 level teaspoons ground cinnamon
pinch of salt
1 cup chopped walnuts (make sure they're fresh and sweet, see Note)
1 cup raisins or sultanas
3 cups grated carrot (usually 3 very large carrots)
1 quantity Lemon Icing (optional) (see following)
finely chopped walnuts (optional)

Preheat the oven to 170°–180°C (325°–350°F). Grease a baking dish or a 28 × 25 × 5 cm large cake tin and line with brown paper and an inner layer of baking paper.

Break the eggs into a large mixing bowl. Add the sugar and give a few stirs with a wooden spoon to start the sugar dissolving. Add the oil, then sift in the flours, bicarbonate of soda, cinnamon and salt. Stir a couple of times with the spoon, then add the walnuts, raisins and carrot. Stir to mix the ingredients evenly, but do not beat.

Pour into prepared baking dish and spread evenly. Bake in the oven for about 1½ hours. Test by inserting a fine skewer into the centre of the cake to make sure it's cooked, then remove from the oven and allow to cool in the tin. Remove from the tin, carefully remove the paper, then ice with Lemon Icing and sprinkle with walnuts (if using).

Walnuts are delicious when fresh, but stale, rancid walnuts can be awful.

Always taste them first before adding to any dish. Canned walnuts are a good item to have on the pantry shelf to ensure freshness.

Lemon Icing

50 g Philadelphia cream cheese
2 level tablespoons soft butter
2 teaspoons fresh lemon juice
finely grated rind of 1 lemon
2 cups icing sugar mixture, sifted

Combine all the ingredients in a mixing bowl or food processor, and beat until smooth and creamy. Use immediately.

Special Birthday Cake

This cake cuts well, so it's ideal for a twenty-first birthday or wedding. For a two-tiered cake to serve 100 people, double the previous recipe and bake in two tins. For the bottom tier, use a 25 × 25 × 9 cm deep tin and bake for about 2 hours. For the top tier, use a small tin 15 × 15 ×7 cm, and bake for about 1–1½ hours.

Lemon Sauce Cake

125 g butter
¾ cup caster sugar
grated rind of 1 lemon
2 eggs
1½ cups self-raising flour
½ cup milk
¼ cup finely chopped blanched almonds

Lemon Sauce
¼ cup fresh lemon juice
¼ cup caster sugar

Preheat the oven to 180°C (350°F). Grease a loaf tin and line the base with baking paper.

Cream the butter and sugar with the lemon rind until light and fluffy. Beat in the eggs one at a time, beating well after each addition. Fold through the flour, then gently stir in the milk and almonds. Put into the prepared loaf tin, spread the mixture to the corners, then give the tin a few sharp taps on the bench to release any large air bubbles (this improves the texture). Bake in the oven for about 50–60 minutes (test by inserting a skewer through one of the surface cracks to make sure it is cooked before removing from the oven).

To make the lemon sauce, combine the lemon juice and caster sugar. Spoon the lemon sauce over the cake while the cake is still hot. Cool slightly, then remove from the tin and cool on a wire rack.

Orange and Almond Cake

Everyone seems to like orange cake and this one is especially moist.

1 heaped teaspoon butter mixed with ½ teaspoon flour, for greasing
185 g butter
¾ cup caster sugar
finely grated rind of 1 orange
3 large eggs
125 g ground almonds (1 cup, firmly packed)
¾ cup self-raising flour, sifted
¼ cup plain flour, sifted
½ cup freshly squeezed orange juice

Preheat the oven to 180°C (350°F). Grease a 22 × 8 cm fancy fluted ring cake tin (7-cup capacity) with the butter and flour mixture (this greasing mixture creates a golden crust).

Cream the butter and sugar until light and fluffy. Add the orange rind, mix through, then beat in the eggs one at a time, beating well after each addition. Add the ground almonds and sifted flours. Mix through evenly, then stir in the orange juice.

Spoon the cake mixture into the prepared cake tin, and bake in the oven for 50–60 minutes. Test by inserting a fine skewer into one of the surface cracks in the cake. Remove from the oven and let stand for 5 minutes, then turn out carefully onto a wire rack. This cake will keep moist for 5 days.

Note: If using a plain 6-cup ring tin, to prevent the cake from overflowing from the tin, hold back a few heaped tablespoons of the mixture and bake some separate muffins or patty cakes.

Cream Scones

Makes 10–14

These scones are soft and moist and very easy to make.

---

2 cups self-raising flour, plus ¼ cup for rolling
½ level teaspoon salt
2 level tablespoons icing sugar mixture
½ cup cream
½ cup milk
1 tablespoon milk, for glazing

Preheat oven to 220°C (425°F). Grease and lightly flour a baking tray or cake tin.

Sift the 2 cups of flour, salt and icing sugar into a mixing bowl. Make a well in the centre and pour in all the cream and milk. Mix quickly into a soft dough, then empty out onto a floured surface and knead lightly with floured hands into a fat round shape (don't knead too much). Turn over so the smooth side is on top and roll out to 2 cm thick (don't roll scones out too thinly, they should be thick). Cut out with a floured 5 or 6 cm scone cutter, then re-roll the scraps two or three times to use all the mixture. Arrange the scones close together on the prepared baking tray. Cover with a clean tea towel and leave to 'rest' for 10 minutes.

Before baking, brush the tops of the scones with milk, then bake in the oven for 15–18 minutes. Remove from the oven, then wrap immediately in a clean tea towel to steam for 5–10 minutes. Serve warm with butter or jam and cream.

Note: Arranging the scones close together in a batch lets them support each other as they rise. They do take a little longer to bake, but they rise well and retain their moisture.

Scones with Tomato and Onion

Comfort food for me is to split open, warm (but not hot), freshly made scones, then top with thin slices of firm, ripe tomato and paper-thin slices of salad onion. Cucumber is also delicious with this combination. Season with pepper and salt, and eat immediately.

Chocolate Slice

Makes 40–50 small squares

Chocolate Cake
2 eggs
²/₃ cup sugar
125 g butter
90 g chocolate, chopped
1 cup plain flour
100 g can walnuts, very finely chopped (always check the walnuts are fresh)
¼ cup milk

Mint Cream Filling
2 level tablespoons soft butter
1 cup sifted icing sugar
1 teaspoon peppermint essence
3 teaspoons boiling water

Chocolate Icing
150 g cooking chocolate, chopped
40 g butter

Preheat the oven to 180°C (350°F). Grease a lamington tin (30 × 20 cm) with butter. To make the cake base, beat the eggs and sugar in the small bowl of an electric mixer until the eggs are frothy. Meanwhile, put the butter and chocolate into a small saucepan and warm gently over a low heat, stirring occasionally. Add this to the egg mixture with the flour and mix through. Stir in the walnuts and milk, then put into the prepared lamington tin. Bake in the oven for about 25 minutes (test with a skewer). Remove from the oven and leave in the tin to cool slightly while making the mint cream filling.

    Beat all the ingredients for the mint cream filling together in a small dish, then spread over the chocolate cake in the tin. Refrigerate to firm the cream while preparing the chocolate icing.

    Put the chocolate into a small heatproof bowl. Add the butter, then melt over warm water, stirring well. Pour over the mint cream layer and spread to the edges. Put in a cool spot (preferably not in the refrigerator as this tends to dull the chocolate). When set, cut into small squares and serve with coffee.

Walnut Crescents

Makes about 6 dozen

These are the biscuits that I make every Christmas to give to friends.

---

250 g butter
½ cup caster sugar
1 teaspoon vanilla essence or extract
1 x 200 g can walnuts
2¼ cups plain flour
1 vanilla bean
sifted icing sugar

Preheat the oven to 180°C (350°F). Lightly grease 3 or 4 baking trays and line with baking paper. Cream the butter, sugar and vanilla essence until light and fluffy. Chop the walnuts in two or three batches in a food processor using the pulse button so you don't over-chop (the nuts should be chopped into a fine meal; be careful that you don't turn them into an oily paste). Add the walnuts to the creamed mixture, then add the flour and mix into a dough.

To shape the biscuits, take small pieces of the dough and roll between the palms of your hands into tapered rolls, and then shape into crescents on the baking tray. If the mixture is too sticky, add an extra tablespoon of flour.

Bake in the oven for about 25 minutes. It takes a little practice to gauge the *exact* cooking time. Make sure you cook them enough so that they are very crisp, but watch carefully during the last 5 minutes of cooking since overcooking can spoil the flavour. Remove from oven and allow to cool.

When completely cold, put the biscuits into an airtight container with the vanilla bean. They will stay fresh and crisp for several weeks providing the container is completely airtight and it's stored in a cool place. When ready to serve or pack into jars for gifts, remove the biscuits from container and place them in a single layer on a sheet of baking paper, then sift over a light drift of icing sugar, turn over and repeat on the other side of biscuit. Don't be too generous with the icing sugar since it can melt during hot weather and be very sticky.

Sauces

Apple Sauce
Lemon Butter
Lime and Ginger Dressing
Mint Sauce
Peanut Sauce
Rich Beef Stock
Jellied Beef Stock
Chicken Stock

Apple Sauce

Makes ¾ cup

3 large Granny Smith apples
¾ cup water
1 level tablespoon sugar
salt and freshly ground black pepper, to taste

Peel, quarter and core apples, then cut into thick slices. Put into a saucepan with the water and sugar. Cover and simmer for 8–10 minutes, or until the apple is tender and fluffy. Season with a tiny pinch of salt and black pepper to taste. Store any leftovers in the refrigerator. Serve with roast pork (see pages 66–67).

Lemon Butter

Makes 4 small jars

This is a lovely lemon butter and it's not too rich or overly sweet.

6 large lemons
150 g butter, cut into squares
2 cups (460 g) plus 2 level tablespoons sugar
6 eggs

Sterilise four small jars with boiling water. Keep hot in a slow oven. Scrub the lemons well under cold, running water, then dry thoroughly. Grate the lemon rind on the fine section of a grater (a pastry brush is handy to remove the rind from the grater). Squeeze the lemons, then strain the juice and put into a saucepan with the lemon rind, butter and sugar. Cook over a low heat, stirring occasionally with a wooden spoon, until the butter melts.

Meanwhile, whisk the eggs lightly in a mixing bowl (just enough to combine yolks and whites). Remove the saucepan from the heat, then gradually add the beaten eggs. Return the saucepan to a very low heat and stir constantly until the mixture thickens and is smooth and shiny.

Pour immediately into the hot, sterilised jars. Seal with a non-metal lid and leave to cool. Store in the refrigerator to keep for 4 weeks. Use as a spread on thick slices of wholemeal bread or as a filling for little pastry tarts, butterfly cakes or sponges.

Lime and Ginger Dressing

Makes ¼ cup

Use this dressing to drizzle over slivers of fresh mango or to dress a mango and cucumber salad.

3 tablespoons fresh lime juice
1 level tablespoon sugar
2 level teaspoons finely grated fresh ginger

Mix the lime juice, sugar and ginger in a small dish, then leave for 10 minutes for the sugar to melt and the flavours to mingle. Use immediately.

Mint Sauce

¼ cup fresh mint leaves, finely chopped
1 tablespoon boiling water
3 tablespoons brown malt vinegar
1½ level tablespoons sugar
pinch of salt
freshly ground black pepper, to taste

Put the mint in a small heatproof jug. Pour over the boiling water to set the colour, then add the vinegar, sugar, salt and pepper, and stir well. Let stand for at least 30 minutes for the flavours to mingle and soften before using.

Peanut Sauce

Makes about 2 cups

1 small onion, peeled and quartered
2 large cloves garlic, peeled
1 thick slice fresh ginger peeled
1 level teaspoon dried chilli flakes
2 tablespoons peanut or light vegetable oil
1 stalk lemon grass (white part)
2 tablespoons tamarind pulp (with seeds)
½ cup (125 mL) hot water
200 g fresh roasted peanuts, ground in a food processor or very finely chopped
1 cup (250 mL) water
1 level tablespoon brown sugar
1 tablespoon Ketjap Manis (Malaysian sweet soy sauce)
juice of 1 lemon

Put the onion, garlic, ginger and chilli flakes into a food processor or blender. Process until mushy, then empty into a heavy frying pan or saucepan, and add the oil. Smash the stem of the lemon grass, then add to the pan. Fry over a low heat, stirring, for about 5 minutes, or until fragrant.

Put the tamarind into a small bowl, pour over the hot water, and work the tamarind with your fingers to dissolve the pulp. Strain the liquid through a sieve, rubbing the sieve to include some of the thick tamarind pulp with the juice.

Add the tamarind to the onion mixture in the pan, then add the peanuts, water, brown sugar and Ketjap Manis. Simmer over a low heat for about 10 minutes, stirring often, until the sauce thickens (add extra water if necessary). Add sufficient lemon juice to suit your taste, then add a little salt if necessary.

Rich Beef Stock

Makes 8 cups (2 litres)

500 g gravy beef
1 veal shank, sawn
1 brown onion, unpeeled
1 large clove garlic
1 carrot, roughly chopped
1 stick celery, roughly chopped
½ cup (125 mL) dry white wine (optional)
12 cups (3 litres) water
bouquet garni (tie a bay leaf, a few sprigs of parsley
and thyme to a piece of celery using white cotton)
black peppercorns

Preheat the oven to 200°C (400°F). Place the gravy beef and veal shank in a greased baking dish. Wash the onion and slice in half (there is no need to peel the onion if the skin is clean and unmarked by mould). Add to the baking dish with the garlic. Bake in the oven for 30 minutes, turning bones once during baking. Add the carrot, celery, and bake for a further 15 minutes.

Transfer to a boiler or a large saucepan, and add the wine (if using), water, bouquet garni and peppercorns (do not add any salt). Cover and simmer slowly for about 3 hours, skimming from time to time as necessary. Strain, then cool the stock quickly by standing the container in a sink filled with cold water. Freeze in recipe-sized quantities. If refrigerated, this stock will keep for up to three days.

Note: All the lovely tender meat from the stock pot can be used to make brawn, (see page 102).

Jellied Beef Stock

This is the secret to success for many a good sauce.

Skim and discard any fat from 4 cups (1 litre) refrigerated Rich Beef Stock (see above). Bring to the boil in a large saucepan or boiler with the lid off. Continue boiling, uncovered, until the stock is concentrated and reduced to about 1 cup (250 mL). Pour into a bowl and refrigerate. The stock will set to a very firm jelly. Use within two days, three at the most. It adds a marvellous unctuous quality to unthickened gravies and sauces.

Chicken Stock

Makes 3 litres

4 chicken frames or 2 kg chicken necks (buy at poultry shop)
2 chicken Marylands (drumstick and thigh)
1 onion, peeled and halved
1 stick celery, halved
½ cup (125 mL) white wine (optional)
16 cups (4 litres) water
1 teaspoon peppercorns
½ bay leaf
few sprigs of fresh parsley
½ teaspoon dried thyme
thin strip of lemon rind

Place all the ingredients in a boiler or large saucepan (do not add any salt). Cover loosely with a lid and simmer for 1½–2 hours. Strain and refrigerate immediately. Skim off any fat from the surface of the stock. Use as required. Any leftover stock should be stored in a labelled airtight container in the freezer. Stir the leftover stock before freezing.

INDEX

Almond Friands 144
Anzac Biscuits 138
Apple Crumble 132
Apple Pie 133
Apple Sauce 154
Avocado Salad, Layered 72

Baked Dinner 56
Banana Fritters 134
Basil Pesto with Pasta 73
Bean and Potato Salad 74
Beef
    Casserole, Rich 40
    Roast Fillet of 38
    Stock, Jellied 157
    Tea 17
Bread and Butter Pudding 127

Caponata 83
Capsicum, Grilled 76
Caramel Syrup 125
Carrot and Potato Fritters 79
Carrot Cake in a Baking Dish 146
Carrots, Glazed Tarragon 78
Carrots, Morrocan 77
Cauliflower Cheese 80
Chicken
    & Noodles, Stir-fried 49
    and Vegetable Soup 14
    Crumbed 45
    Curry, Thai 48
    Italian Roast 44
    Juicy Roast Tarragon 46
    Pie 50
    Stock 15, 158
    Teriyaki 100
Chickpea Salad, Spiced 75
Chilli Plum Sauce 107
Chocolate Cake, Double 145
Chocolate Chip Biscuits 139
Chocolate Slice 151
Corn Flapjacks, Mini 81

Couscous 84
Crème Brûlée 121
Custard, Vanilla Egg 122
Custard, Boiled Vanilla 123

Eggs Benedict 112
Eggs, Fluffy Scrambled 114
Eggplant, Sam's Baked 82

Fish and Chips 34
Fish Curry 36
French Caramel Apple Pudding 130
French Onion Soup 13
Fruit Salad, Summer 136

Ginger Sponge *see* Upside-down Pear Cake, Gwen's
Gingerbread Biscuits, My Favourite 140
Golden Syrup Dumplings 119
Green Salad, Favourite 95
Greek Prawns with Feta 32
Greek Roast Lamb with Lemon 52
Guacamole 110

Hirira 18
Hummus bi Tahini 108
Hummus, David's Easy 109
Hollandaise Sauce, Microwave 112

Irish Stew 53

Jam Drops 142
Jam Roly, Baked Apricot 118

Kedgeree 101

Laksa Lemak, Quick and Easy 20
Lamb

Chop and Potato Bake 58
Curry 54
Shank and Barley Broth 16
Soup *see* Hirira
Roast *see* Baked Dinner with Lemon, Greek Roast 52
Shepherd's Pie 59
Lasagne, Easy 62
Lemon Butter 154
Lemon Delicious 120
Lemon Sauce Cake 148
Lime and Ginger Dressing 155

Macaroni Cheese 104
Marmalade Pudding, Steamed 128
Meat Balls in Tomato Sauce, Margaret's 63
Meat Pie, My Mother's 42
Melting Moments, Joy's 143
Mince, Savoury 60
Mint Sauce 155
Mornay, Scallop Prawn 28
Mushrooms on Toast 85

Nuoc Cham 90

Olive Oil Mash 90
Orange and Almond Cake 149

Paella, Seafood 26
Pancakes, Lemon 116
Panna Cotta 124
Pastry, Crunchy Shortcrust 133
Pea and Ham Soup 12
Peanut Sauce 156
Pie Pastry, Special 43
Pilaf Rice, Turkish 96
Pizza, Easy No-yeast 105
Polenta with Mushrooms and Tomatoes, Soft 86

Polenta, Soft 87
Pork in Satay Sauce 65
Pork Sausages in Tomato and
    Cumin Gravy 64
Pork with Crackling, Roast 66
Potato
    and Celeriac Mash 89
    and Leek Soup 10
    Bake, Farmer's 92
    Chips 35
    Gratin 91
    in Fresh Tomato Sauce,
        Coriander 93
    Mashed 88
    Salad, Creamy 94
Prawn and Fresh Herb Risotto 24
Prawn Soup, Thai Hot and
    Sour 21
Prawn Stock 21, 158
Prawns with Fetta, Greek 32
Pumpkin and Leek Soup,
    Butternut 10
Pumpkin Soup 11

Rhubarb and Apple 135
Rice Pudding, Creamy 129
Ricotta with Gremolata,
    Baked 111
Risotto, Prawn and Fresh Herb 24

Salmon Patties 30
Sauce
    Apple 154
    Bechamel (with Cheese) 62
    Bernaise 38
    Bolognaise 61
    Chilli Plum 107
    Hollandaise, Microwave 112
    Lemon Butter 154
    Lime and Ginger Dressing 155
    Mint 57, 155
    Nouc Cham 107
    Peanut 156
    Tartare 35
Scallop and Prawn Mornay 28
Scones, Cream 150
Scones, with Tomato and
    Onion 150
Shepherd's Pie 59
Shepherd's Salad 97
Spring Rolls, Vietnamese
    Fresh 106
Soup
    Beef Tea 17
    Butternut Pumkin and Leek 10
    Chicken and Vegetable 14
    French Onion 13
    Hirira 18
    Lamb Shank and Barley
        Broth 16

Pea and Ham 12
Potato and Leek 10
Pumpkin 11
Quick and Easy Laksa
    Lemak 20
Tom Yum Goon 21
Won Ton Soup 22
Spaghetti Bolognaise 61
Stock
    Chicken 15,158
    Jellied Beef 157
    Prawn 21, 158
    Rich Beef 157
Swordfish, Char-grilled 33

Tomato and Basil Salad 98
Trifle, Apple and Blackcurrant 117
Tuna and Fresh Coriander
    Patties 31

Upside-down Pear Cake,
    Gwen's 126

Veal and Ham Brawn 102
Veal and Mushroom Stew 69
Veal Casserole 68
Veal with Mushroom Sauce,
    Pot Roast of 70

Walnut Crescents 152
Won Ton Soup 22
Won Ton Dumplings 22